£2·00
29/5/92

Vanessa Keegan's
MACHINE KNITTING BOOK

100

£1

MR. MUHAMMADALI. BJUR HONS.MJUR
ADVOCATE · PRE ADD - 63A HART ROAD
- BENFLEET · ESSEX · UK - SS7-3PB.
- MOB - 07961827360 -
PER. ADD - ROWSONARA BEGUM
- (MOTER) - ISLAMPUR - DEVISING
PARA P.O. KAJLA - P.S. MOTIHAR
- DIST- DHAKA - RAJSHAHICITY
- BANGLADES -
TEL. 00880721- 750564 -

Vanessa Keegan's
MACHINE KNITTING BOOK

OVER 30 ORIGINAL DESIGNS
Photography by Pablo Keller

CENTURY
London Melbourne Auckland Johannesburg

For Mum and Marcus

First published in 1988 by Century Hutchinson Ltd,
Brookmount House, 62-65 Chandos Place,
Covent Garden,
London WC2N 4NW

Century Hutchinson Australia Pty Ltd,
PO Box 496, 16-22 Church Street, Hawthorn,
Victoria 3122, Australia

Century Hutchinson New Zealand Ltd,
PO Box 40-086, Glenfield, Auckland 10,
New Zealand
Century Hutchinson South Africa Pty Ltd,
PO Box 337, Bergvlei, 2012 South Africa

Design: Clare Clements
Editors: Sue Hopper and Anne Smith
Stylist: John Walton
Photographic Production Manager: Marcus Tate
Make-up Artist: Katya Thomas
Artwork: Anthony Duke, Stephen Duke,
Colin Salmon, Taurus Graphics and Lindsay Blow

Set in Grot 126/215/216
by SX Composing Ltd, Rayleigh, Essex

Printed and bound in Spain
by Printer industria gráfica s.a Barcelona

British Library Cataloguing in Publication Data

Keegan, Vanessa
  Vanessa Keegan machine knitting book:
  over 30 original designs
  1. Machine knitting-Pattern
  I. Title
  746.43'2041

ISBN 0 7126 1182 7

Contents

PREFACE 8

TECHNICAL HINTS 9

BLITHE SPIRIT 15

Linear 19
A contemporary Fair Isle is achieved using three colours. If you want to accentuate this look, try changing the colours of the stripes.

Zigzag 21
The classic Fair Isle pullover, given a new look. Knit it in cotton, or in warmer woollen colours for winter.

Child's Zigzag 23
A pretty sweater using the same pattern as the pullover. For a boy, simply change the colours.

Domino 26
This cropped sweater tapers slightly at the waist, with an unusual square neckline and wide sleeves tapering down to the cuff.

Diamonds 29
Knitted in cotton, with short sleeves and a band of black diamonds above the body ribs and along the sleeve tops.

TRANSATLANTIC 31

Babe Ruth 32
This two-toned cardigan can be worn with the skirt as a suit or on its own. It has two practical pockets, contrasting sleeves and ribs.

Babe Ruth Skirt 35
This skirt is a feminine alternative to the baseball image, and is simple to make.

Baseball 36
A practical cardigan with obvious references to the classic baseball jacket. The inset collar stripe also appears on the ribs.

Eldorado 39
All the romance of the classic Caddy. You could easily use this chart in conjunction with a basic adult's pattern.

Trucking 42
This design takes a lot of patience to produce, but the finished effect is always treasured.

New Jersey 47
Dynamic sports sweater in cotton or wool. It can be made with either a collar or crew neck.

DOWN TO EARTH 49

Shetland 51
The two flecked yarns create a subtle blending of colours, enhanced by the fringe pattern. The V-neck, with overlapping inset collar, can be turned down or left snug around the neck.

Shetland Skirts 55
Two simple and practical skirts which complement the Shetland sweaters.

Fish Bone 56
This repeated fish-bone pattern works with almost any background colour. Knitted in a cotton yarn, it would make a cool spring sweater.

Carrots 61
Oversized and warm for winter, the stylized carrot creates a stencilled effect. If desired, change the background colour, keeping the pattern dark.

Windfall 63
This leaf motif cardigan has two handy pockets and a V-neck. The narrow front ribs are knitted in two pieces, joining at the centre back.

Windfall Dress 66
A simple dress slightly shaped at the waist, with turnover collar and deep armholes narrowing to cuffs.

ETHNOGRAPHIC 69

Braided Zigzag 73
Can be worn as a dress or oversized sweater, belted or straight. You could alter the length by omitting a zigzag repeat.

Block Print 75
Traditional shape with an unconventional pattern, comfortable crew neck and armholes. This design is most successful with a neutral background.

Lotus 78
This design is derived from the lotus flower. Keeping the background neutral, you could use alternative colours in the patterning.

Lotus Child 81
A scaled-down version of the adult's Lotus sweater, making a warm and practical sweater for a boy or girl.

Diamond Dress 84
A warm winter dress worn belted or straight. The length can be altered by omitting a sequence of the diamond repeat.

Rough Diamond 87
A colourful, relaxed woollen cardigan with practical pockets, ideal for winter, or, alternatively, in cotton with paler colours for spring.

SUMMER CLASSICS 91

Black & White 93
This sweater is most successful in a yarn which allows it to drape. It has a boat neck with collar and narrower stripes at the sleeve inset.

Tea Rose 95
This simple, cabled camisole top is perfect for summer, and makes a practical twin-set when worn with the Tea Rose Cardigan.

Tea Rose Cardigan 97
This traditional cardigan with pockets and small neat ribs also has three rows of cables running down the centre back. Glass buttons enhance its antique feel.

Silk Skirt 100
This slender skirt is simple to make. The length can be altered by adding or omitting rows. It could also be worn with the Tea Rose Cardigan.

Cabled Silk 101
A simple top with a series of narrow cables around the neck. Worn on its own or with the skirt, it is easily made in a beautiful silk yarn.

Metropolitan 103
The use of silk and wool mixed yarn gives this sweater dress an interesting surface. It works best in fairly neutral colours using different shades of the same colour.

WINTER CLASSICS 105

Squares 107
A simple, effective pattern using flecked wool. Random squares are selected in different colours.

Short Squares 109
This is a cropped version of the man's Squares sweater. It is in a reverse colourway with randomly selected squares.

Oak Leaf 112
This Oak Leaf sleeveless cardigan has a plain back with fine ribs, two small pockets and an optional half belt.

WOMAN'S WORK 115

Washing Up 116
This expressive polka dot cup design creates the impression of flying crockery. The collar gives an alternative neck detail.

Cleaning Up 119
The archetypal domestic vacuum cleaner of the '50s was the inspiration for this pattern.

Maternity Leave 122
This simple embryonic spiral creates a paisley effect, keeping its light-hearted title ambiguous.

Ironing Out 125
The graphic treatment of the classic iron gives the sweater its title. For a more restrained feel, knit this motif sweater with a neutral background colour.

ACKNOWLEDGEMENTS 128

YARN SUPPLIERS 128

Preface

8 Edith Sitwell once wrote of Virginia Woolf 'I enjoyed talking to her, but thought nothing of her writing. I considered her a beautiful little knitter.' The association of 'knitter' with the diminutive 'little' illustrates precisely how knitting has been downgraded as a form of expression primarily because most of its practitioners are women. However, in recent years, interest in hand-knitting and the many diverse hand-knit publications have encouraged and inspired both practised knitters and those wishing to learn the craft. Machine knitting, on the other hand, has always been its rather unglamorous sister: many potential knitters confident enough to buy the machines in the first place have quickly lost interest because of the uninspiring patterns and lack of encouragement. I hope this book will help to redress the balance.

The main advantage of machine knitting is obviously speed, although this is not an end in itself. It is in the design process where its main attraction lies. Machine knitting frees creative energy and enables the quick exploration of ideas. In my experience, designs which have taken a lot of time and effort to make, but which in the end are not successful, are not easily discarded.

Many newcomers to the knitting machine are daunted by it, yet the machines are relatively simple and robust, so try not to be inhibited by the machine itself. By starting with a simple design, you will gradually begin to master all the technical ramifications.

There is enormous satisfaction to be gained from producing a sweater for yourself, a friend or a relation, and I have tried to ensure that whatever the ability of the knitter, there is a selection of patterns available. Whether you simply want to make a sweater as instructed, or prefer instead to use a pattern as a starting point for altering or creating your own designs, I hope this book conveys my enthusiasm for the relatively unexplored art of machine knitting. Some of these designs have been sold ready-made to discerning high-fashion shops, so it gives me a lot of satisfaction to enable the knitter to make them at a fraction of that cost, and thus reach a larger audience.

Vanessa Keegan
April 1988

Technical Hints

BEFORE YOU START
Machines

On a knitting machine, the distance between the needles within the bed determines which thickness of yarn can be knitted on it: this is called the gauge. Fine-gauge machines are used for knitting fine industrial-type yarns, standard-gauge machines for knitting anything from 2 ply (fingering) to a fine double knitting (knitted worsted) weight, and chunky machines for the more usual hand-knitting and fancy yarns.

All the garments in this book have been knitted on standard-gauge machines, and each pattern states which type of machine is needed to produce a particular stitch pattern.

The simpler, plain and striped garments can be made on any basic model. These machines are usually bought by the beginner who wants a moderately priced machine to learn on, the very simplest machine starting at around £80 ($128). They are able to knit simple patterns by selecting the needles, either manually or by pressing buttons, on every row.

Next come the punchcard models, which can produce all-over repeating patterns or single motifs. The pattern is first punched, as holes, on to a plastic sheet and then fed into the machine.

These machines restrict you to a set number of stitches, generally 24, across the width of the pattern.

Finally, in the higher price range of around £800 ($1,280) or more, come the electronic machines. These are far more complicated to learn but have the advantage that patterns can be worked over any number of stitches up to 60 in width. The patterns for these machines are simply marked on to special sheets of paper, using the pen provided.

On all the garments in this book the ribbed welts (ribbings), cuffs, collars and borders have been made by using a ribbing attachment, but, as this is quite an expensive optional extra, all the patterns include instructions on how to work them on a single-bed machine.

The two children's sweaters, Eldorado and Trucking, have been knitted using the intarsia technique. Not all machines can do this without a special intarsia carriage, so check your instruction manual to see if an extra attachment is needed.

Before following any of the patterns, check with your instruction manual whether the techniques given in the pattern are correct for your machine. If you are following a punchcard pattern, for example, you may not need to set the carriage one row before starting to knit the pattern; if you do, you may drop some of the stitches. Also, on some of the older punchcard machines the background and second colours are reversed so that the holes punched in the card represent the background colour.

If you are not sure which techniques are right for your machine, knit a small swatch of the stitch pattern first to see which settings you should use to achieve the desired result – this swatch can then be used to check your tension.

Yarn

Within each pattern yarns have been specified for use in making your garment. If you use the correct yarn and achieve the correct tension, you should be completely satisfied with the completed garment.

If you cannot easily obtain the correct yarn, you can substitute a yarn of similar thickness. To do this satisfactorily, check first on the approximate thickness of the yarn, the tension it knits to, and the composition.

If you are not sure, see if you can purchase a small amount of the yarn first in order to try it out and compare it with the look of the yarn in the picture. Check to see that it knits to the correct tension without looking so loose that the garment will not hold its shape or so tight that it will not hang correctly. Finally, remember that the quantities stated are approximate and that if you use a different yarn, the amount of the yarn you choose could vary quite considerably from that quoted.

Tension

All the measurements of each garment have been calculated according to the number of stitches and rows worked to a given tension. This means that if the pattern quotes 27 stitches and 39 rows to 10 cm (4 in) measured over stocking (stockinette) stitch with a tension-dial setting of approximately 7, it is vital that you achieve the tension of 27 stitches and 39 rows, although the tension-

Abbreviations

alt	alternate(ly)
beg	beginning
cm	centimetre(s)
cont	continu(e)(ing)
dec	decreas(e)(ing)
foll	following
g	grams
HP	holding position
in	inch(es)
inc	increas(e)(ing)
K	knit
mm	millimetres
MT	main tension
MT−1, MT−2, MT−3	one, two or three full sizes tighter than main tension
MT+1, MT+2, MT+3	one, two or three full sizes looser than main tension
MY	main yarn
NWP	non-working position
N	needles
oz	ounces
P	purl
patt	pattern
RC	row counter
rem	remain(ing)
rep	repeat
st(s)	stitch(es)
st st	stocking stitch (stockinette stitch)
tog	together
UWP	upper working position
WP	working position
WY	waste yarn

Advice for American knitters

Most of the terms in this book are the same in English and American terminology. The main differences are between the metric and imperial measurements and weights. Where appropriate, the imperial measurements and weights have been given after the metric ones within every pattern.

The terms which vary are given with their equivalents below:

10

UK	US
cast off	bind off
slipstitch	tack down
stocking stitch	stockinette stitch
tension	gauge
4 ply	sport
double knitting	knitting worsted
Aran	fisherman
chunky	bulky
colourway(s)	choice of colour(s)

dial setting is not so important and could be as low as 5 or as high as 9 as long as it produces the correct tension.

When working a tension swatch, always cast on at least 10 more stitches and work at least 10 more rows than quoted in the tension specified to give an accurate reading.

Punchcards and charts

On the patterned garments in this book it is necessary to punch the designs on to a punchcard or mark up on to the special sheets for the electronic machines.

Most punchcard machines have the contrast colour as the one which is translated into the holes on the card, but check with your instruction manual to see if this is true of your machine. There is usually a minimum number of rows required in order that the punchcard can be formed into a circle and clipped together. Again check with your instruction book, and if the pattern repeat does not give enough rows, then just punch the pattern twice in order to give enough rows. Always take note, perhaps when working your tension sample, of the row number marked on the punchcard that signals that the first row of pattern is to be knitted. Different machines need a different number of rows for the card to be wound into the machine before the punched holes are read, and if the correct make of punchcard is not easily available for your machine, then the card you use may not necessarily show row 1 when the first row of pattern is about to be knitted.

Electronic machines differ from punchcard machines in the way they set and read the pattern. They also give far more choice in that, at the flick of a switch, the pattern can be reversed, turned upside down or have the colours reversed. Again,

check with your instruction manual whether a minimum number of rows is required for the pattern and also whether it needs to be marked in reverse, as with the punchcard machines.

You will see throughout this book that all the charts seem to be the wrong way round to the pattern on the garments. This is because you always work with the back of the work facing you. As soon as you turn the work the right way round, the patterns will look the same as in the pictures.

There can be no hard and fast rules for marking up a punchcard or pattern sheet, as new models are coming on to the market all the time, so if you have any questions, please follow the only rule that is always true: check with the instruction manual for your machine.

Floats

A few of the garments have large colour patterns which leave long floats on the inside of the fabric. Although they have been kept to a minimum, these can be a nuisance, especially in the sleeves.

If you are afraid that these floats might catch and spoil the look of your garment, there are two methods of dealing with them. The first is to use iron-on interfacing fabric to cover the floats, although this can be a little bit tricky to put on properly. The second is to use thread matching the main yarn and catch (tack) down the floats to the inside of the garment at regular intervals.

Measurements

The measurements on the diagrams and patterns are given throughout in both centimetres and inches. The figures in brackets refer to the larger sizes; if only one figure is given, then this refers to all sizes.

TECHNIQUES
Casting on
There are two main methods of casting on in machine knitting. The first is the nylon-cord method, which is very quick and easy but leaves an unfinished edge and so is only suitable for tension swatches, stitch samples or casting on with waste yarn when making a hem. The second is the closed-edge method, which is a little slower, but gives a neat finished edge that resembles the hand-knit method of casting on.

Casting on with nylon cord

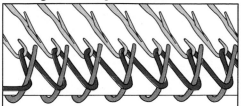

1. Bring forward the required number of needles to working position. Thread the carriage with the main yarn and set the tension slightly looser than the main tension for the yarn. Holding the end of the yarn from the carriage down below the needlebed, move the carriage from right to left over the needles so that the main yarn forms a zigzag between the hooks on the needles and the sinker posts.

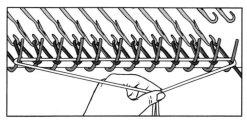

2. Take out the nylon cord, supplied with the machine, and lay it over the zigzag formed by the main yarn, making sure that it passes between the needle hooks and the sinker posts. Hold both ends of the nylon cord firmly with the left hand beneath the needlebed, pulling it tightly against the main yarn. Set the tension to main tension.

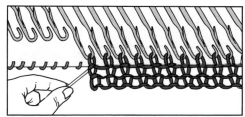

3. Set the machine to knit all the needles, and knit about six rows. Carefully pull out the nylon cord from one end, then continue to knit as required.

Casting on with a closed edge

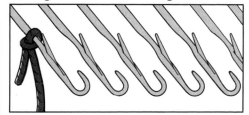

1. Bring forward the required number of needles to holding position. Set the machine to knit all the needles and the tension to main tension. Thread the carriage with the main yarn and make a slip loop near the end of the yarn. Place this loop over the needle furthest away from the carriage.

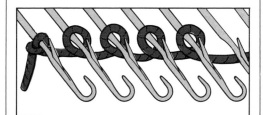

2. Holding the main yarn in your right hand, wind it anticlockwise round each needle, working from left to right. When winding the yarn, keep it fairly loose; otherwise, the loops formed on the needles will not knit properly when the carriage is passed over them. When the yarn has been wound round all the needles, pull back the yarn through the tension mast to take up any slackness, then knit the row. Continue knitting as required.

Casting off (Binding off)
The two most common methods of casting off are taking the fabric off on to waste yarn and the transfer-tool method. The first is quick and simple, ideal for tension swatches and stitch samples, or when stitches are to be picked up again at a later stage in making the garment. The second method is used when shaping at a neck or armhole, or if a closed, finished edge is required.

Casting off with waste yarn

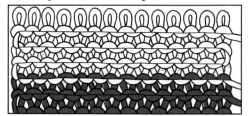

On completion of the required number of rows in main yarn, break off the yarn and unthread the carriage. Rethread the carriage with a contrasting yarn of similar thickness to the main yarn, and knit about six rows. Break off the contrast yarn and unthread the carriage. Remove any weights from the work. Then, supporting the fabric with your free hand, run the carriage once across the stitches, causing them to 'drop off' the needles. The waste yarn will hold the stitches in main yarn securely until required later.

Casting off (binding off) with a transfer tool
On completion of the required number of rows in the main yarn, end with the carriage at the right-hand side of the needlebed.

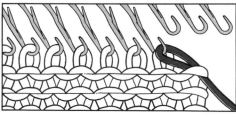

1. Using the single transfer tool, move the first stitch at the right-hand side on to the adjacent needle to the left, so that there are two stitches on this needle. Push the empty needle back into non-working position.

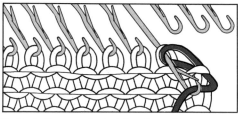

2. Push the needle holding two stitches forward so that both stitches lie behind the latch, leaving the latch in the open position. Take the yarn from the carriage in your left hand and lay it loosely across the hook, then close the latch over the yarn.

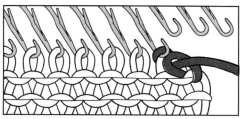

3. Holding the needle butt in your right hand, gently draw the loop of yarn in the needle hook through the two stitches behind the latch, then place the needle back into working position.

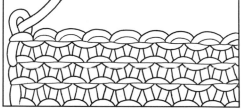

4. Repeat steps 1 to 3 until the required number of stitches have been cast off. If you are casting off all the stitches, break the yarn and thread it through last stitch, pulling up tightly to secure. In order to prevent the stitches being cast off too tightly, and to give an even finish, pass the yarn used for casting off in front of the sinker post between each cast-off stitch. This will have the effect of holding the knitting on the machine until the casting off is complete, when it can then be carefully lifted off.

11

Hems and ribs

All the garments in this book have had the welts (ribbings), cuffs and borders knitted on a machine with a ribbing attachment. Alternatively, on a single bed machine the ribs can be worked as a mock rib him, or hand knitted.

2 × 1 mock rib hem

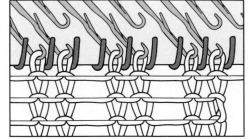

1. Bring forward to working position the required number of needles, as given in the pattern, for the piece of knitting after the rib has been knitted. Push every third needle back to non-working position. Cast on with waste yarn and work six rows, then change to main yarn and a tension approximately two numbers tighter than main tension and work enough rows to form twice the depth of the completed hem.

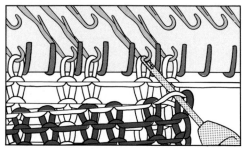

2. Fold the hem in half, allowing the waste yarn to roll forward. Using the single transfer tool, pick up the short loop between the first two stitches in the first row of main yarn and place it on to the second needle in working position.

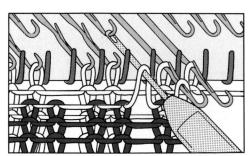

3. * Pick up the next loop – this is a longer loop formed where the needle was pushed back into non-working position – and place on to the next needle without a stitch. Pick up the next short loop: then, missing the next needle, place this loop on to the following needle. Repeat from * to end of row, placing the last loop on to the last needle. Change to main tension and continue knitting the pattern. The waste yarn can be removed either straight away or at the end of the piece of knitting.

Hand-knit ribs

When hand-knitting ribs, cast on the required number of stitches using needles about two sizes smaller than those which are recommended for hand knitting on the yarn that you are using.

Work in rib for the correct depth, ending with a right-side row.

Bring forward the required number of needles to working position, then, with the wrong side of the rib facing and using the single transfer tool, hook each stitch individually on to the knitting machine needles, letting each one drop off the hand-knitting needle.

How to pick up dropped stitches

If a stitch is accidentally dropped, it can very quickly run down and form a ladder, especially if there are weights hanging on the knitting, but it is quite easily picked up again using the latch tool.

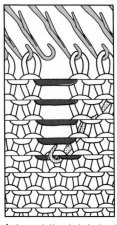 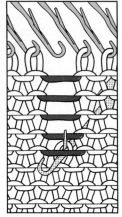

1. Insert the latch tool, from behind the knitting, into the stitch below the dropped stitch taking care not to split it.
2. Gently pull down on the knitting so that it unravels to the stitch on the hook.* Push the latch hook towards you through the fabric so that the stitch lies behind the latch and the latch is open, then catch the bar from the row above in the hook of the latch tool.

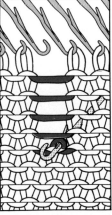 

3. Pulling down gently on the fabric, draw the new stitch through.
4. Repeat from * until the final bar has been picked up, then, using the single transfer tool, hook the stitch back on to the empty needle and continue with the knitting.

Increasing and decreasing

In order to work shaping on a garment, for example, to increase the fabric along the side of the sleeve or to decrease the fabric at the neck or armhole, then increasing or decreasing needs to be worked. On both techniques, either a simple manoeuvre can be performed using a single transfer tool, or a method called fully fashioned shaping can be used. The choice is purely personal, although most patterns suggest which method to use. If the pattern just tells you to increase or decrease without specifying the method, then it is generally accepted that the simple method is to be used.

Simple increasing

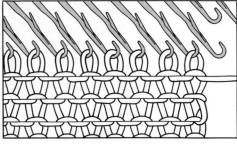

At the same end of the needlebed as the carriage, bring forward one needle to working position. Knit the row by passing the carriage across the needles. The empty needle will have caught the yarn as it passes across and formed a stitch.

Fully fashioned increasing

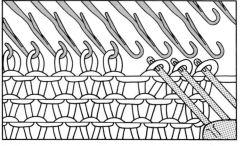

1. At either end of the needlebed and using the triple transfer tool, move the first three stitches one needle outwards. This leaves the fourth needle without a stitch.

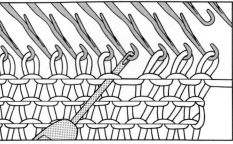

2. Insert the single transfer tool through the top of the stitch below the stitch on the fifth needle and place this loop on to the empty needle to prevent a hole forming when the row is knitted.

Simple decreasing

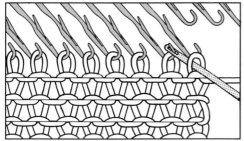

At either end of the needlebed, take the first stitch on to the single transfer tool and move it on to the second needle in. Push the empty needle back into non-working position.

Fully fashioned decreasing

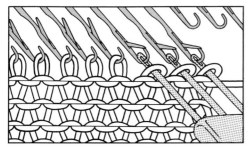

1. At either end of the needlebed, take the first three stitches on to the triple transfer tool, being careful not to drop one.

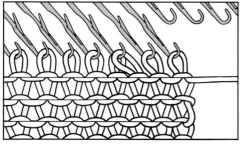

2. Move these three stitches one needle in, so that there are two stitches on the third needle. Push the empty needle back into non-working position.

Making up

Making up is just as important a part of making a garment as knitting it. Beautiful pieces of knitted fabric can be ruined by not taking enough time and trouble in sewing them together.

Once all the pieces have been knitted, it is essential that all loose ends, from joining in new balls of yarn or changing colour, are darned in securely and trimmed off. Do not cut the ends too short, or when the garment is worn the slightest movement will stretch the fabric and pull the ends out; then your garment could start to unravel.

Blocking and pressing

All of the garment patterns at this point suggest that the pieces are pinned out and pressed or steamed according to the directions on the ball or cone band. This is optional and purely a matter of personal preference. If you find it difficult to sew up the pieces when they are curling, then block

and press the pieces. If you are at all unsure, and are afraid of damaging the fabric, test a sample swatch first or make up the pieces without blocking and pressing.

Blocking

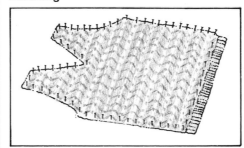

Place a thick layer of blanket on to a flat surface and cover with a smooth cloth. Lay out each piece of the garment, checking the measurements from the diagram, and pin out to size, leaving the ribbing unpinned.

If the yarn can be pressed, then either press the pieces under a damp cloth or steam them gently without placing any pressure on the fabric.

If the yarn cannot be pressed, place a damp cloth over the pinned-out fabric and leave until completely dry. Do not block or press ribbing.

Finishing the neckband

For a really professional finish to a neckband, fold the neckband in half on to the right side of the garment and backstitch the open stitches into position, using the same colour yarn.

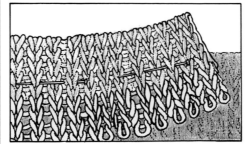

1. Fold the neckband in half on to the right side of the garment and pin into position.

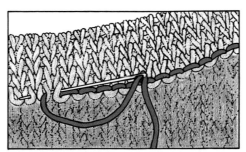

2. Thread a blunt-ended needle with matching yarn and join at beginning of neckband. Unravelling the waste yarn carefully as you work, backstitch through each individual stitch to the end of the neckband. Fasten off securely.

Joining the pieces

When sewing the pieces together, invisible stitch is the best stitch to use for sewing the straight seams because it is worked from the right side of the fabric and each stitch can be matched; this is very important if there are stripes or stitch patterns at the seams. For sewing curved seams, a backstitch seam is the strongest, and again it is not too difficult to match any necessary stripes or patterns.

Invisible stitch

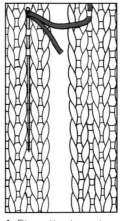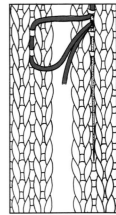

13

1. Place the two pieces to be joined side by side with the right sides facing up. Thread a blunt-ended needle with matching yarn and join at top of seam. Insert the needle under two horizontal threads, one stitch in, on the first piece.
2. * Draw the needle through, then pick up the corresponding two threads on the second piece.

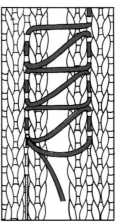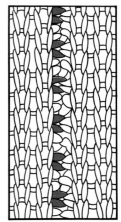

3. Draw the needle through, then return to the first piece and pick up the next two threads. Repeat from * several times more.
4. Gently pull the thread to close the seam. Repeat again from step 2 to the end of the seam, then fasten off securely.

Backstitch seam

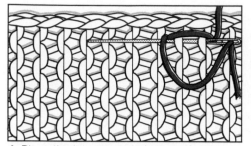

1. Place the two pieces to be joined with right sides together. Thread a blunt ended needle with matching yarn and join at beginning of seam.

14

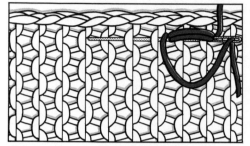

2. Insert the needle back through both thicknesses of fabric, a little to the right of the first stitch, then bring up the same distance to the left of the first stitch.

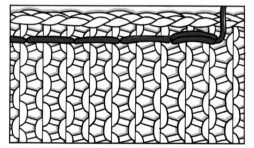

3. * Insert the needle back through the fabric where the stitch before last came out, then bring back out the same distance to the left of the last stitch. Repeat from * to the end of the seam, then fasten off securely.

Cables

Cables are easy to work on a knitting machine. To create the method most hand knitters use, with a purl stitch running down each side of the cable, it is necessary to have a double-bed machine or ribbing attachment. Cables worked in stocking stitch on a single bed machine can look equally effective.

When working a cable, you need to refer to the pattern to find out which needles to work the cable over and whether to use double or triple-transfer tools.

To make a cable

1. Knit to the position of the first cable twist. * Pick up the first set of stitches on to the first transfer tool and hold these in one hand; take the second transfer tool and place the second set of stitches on to it, and hold it in the other hand.

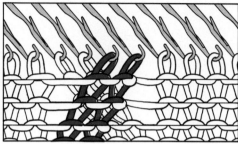

2. Cross the transfer tools left over right or right over left as given in the pattern, then place each set of stitches back on to the empty needles, thus changing the position of the stitches. Knit the required number of rows, then repeat from * for the number of times required.

Adding a third colour

Sometimes the overall effect of a pattern is greatly improved if a third colour is used within the row. It is not possible to do this automatically as with two colours, but providing it is only needed over a few stitches, as in the Squares sweaters, it is quite easy to do as follows:

Using the usual two-colour pattern method, knit the required number of rows to the position where a third colour is needed. With the carriage to the right or left of the needlebed, push forward to holding position the needles on which the third colour is to be knitted. Knit the row with the two colours threaded into the machine. Now, with the third colour, knit back the needles in holding position by hand. Then if necessary, reset the needles into holding position ready for the next row.

Continue in this way on every row where a third colour is required, then break off the yarn and continue knitting in the normal way.

Intarsia

This is a special method of knitting where you can use as many colours in the row as you wish, giving you complete control over the pattern. It is ideal for large motifs and picture knitting. In order to work this technique, you must either have a machine with a special intarsia carriage or one which is able to knit a row of stitches and then

automatically leave the needles further forward than the normal working position, with all the stitches lying just behind the open latches.

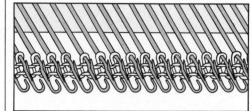

1. Knit to position for start of the motif. Then, before working the last row, set the machine so that the needles move forward, when knitted, with all the stitches lying behind the latches. Knit the row.

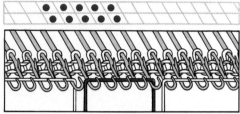

2. Unthread the yarn from the tension mast assembly and carriage. Working from a chart for the pattern and with the balls or cones of yarn on the floor beside you (in front of the machine), lay the yarns over the needles in the direction that the carriage is going to knit and in order of colours and number of stitches that you wish them to knit. For small areas of colour, it is easier to work with short lengths of yarn instead of balls or cones.

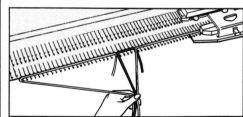

3. Holding the ends of the yarns loosely in the left hand, pass the carriage across the needles. Each colour yarn should have knitted back over the needles over which it was lying.

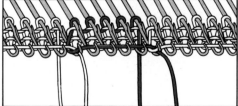

4. Lay the yarns back over the needles in the opposite direction, twisting each yarn round the next colour in between the needles in order to stop a hole forming. Knit the row. Continue in this way, gradually building up the motif until it has been completed. Break off all the yarns. Set the machine for normal knitting. Then thread up the tension mast and carriage and continue to knit.

Blithe Spirit

To create an echo of the Thirties, I used the colours of English china from that period. In fact, decorative china is a wonderful and seemingly inexhaustible design resource. Using these greyed pastels in a silky mercerized cotton yarn inevitably gives the sweaters a traditional look.

The patterns also look attractive in bright primary colours, in which case you might want to use an unmercerized cotton to give a more contemporary look. For instance, try knitting the Linear pattern in orange or red with a black zig zag line. I prefer an ecru or off-white for the background rather than a bleached white, so the contrast is not so stark.

The Diamond sweater has one band of black diamonds at the rib on the front and back, and across the sleeve tops. This of course could be omitted. Alternatively, you can accentuate the band by alternating the colour of the diamonds all the way up the sweater. Try changing the colour every half diamond; knit a few experimental swatches and extend the design according to your preference. This sweater can be easily shortened by omitting a band or two of diamonds and adjusting the pattern.

Both the Diamond and the Domino patterns are worked out with positive and negative interlinking images. This treatment is interesting with many different geometric shapes. It's important to realize that you need to break up the hard edge of the shape with alternate stitches – otherwise the knitting will separate, creating a ladder effect. The Domino sweater tapers slightly at the waist and has wide sleeves tapering down to the cuff. It also has an unusual square neckline with narrow ribs and needs careful invisible stitching on the overlapping corners when attaching the rib-side edge to the sweater.

The Zigzag pattern has a traditional Fair Isle effect because of its scale and also because it uses the technique of swapping the ground colour behind the motif (in this case the dash). This gives the illusion of having more than two colours in a row. To exaggerate the Fair Isle look, change the colour of the stripe alternately or throughout the sweater. The man's Zigzag pullover is patterned on the back, but to knit it plain remember to adjust yarn requirements.

When designing these small geometric shapes, rhythm – the spacing between the positive and negative areas – is important. Designing simple patterns can be surprisingly difficult – often it's much harder to be economical with pattern structure and colour – so, if you want to start designing your own patterns, keep them as simple as you can.

A contemporary Fair Isle effect, achieved with only three colours. To accentuate this look, use more colours and change the stripe colour sequentially.

PATTERN RATING
● ● ● For fairly experienced knitters.

MACHINES
This pattern is suitable for standard gauge punchcard machines.

MATERIALS
Rowan Cabled Mercerised Cotton.
275 [300, 325] g (10[11, 12] oz) in shade 301 (MC).
170 [175, 180] g (6[6½, 6½] oz) in shade 310 (A).
95 [100, 105] g (3½[4, 4] oz) in shade 319 (B).
Rowan Cabled Mercerised Cotton is 100% Pure Cotton.

YARN THICKNESS
Medium yarn.

MEASUREMENTS
To fit chest 76-82 [87-92, 97-102] cm, 30-32 [34-36, 38-40] in.
Actual measurement 103 [113, 123] cm, 40½ [44½, 48½] in.
Length to shoulder 54.5 cm, 21½ in.
Sleeve seam 18.5 cm, 7¼ in.
Instructions are written for the smallest size, larger sizes follow in square brackets. If only one figure is given, it applies to all sizes.

TENSION
30 stitches and 38 rows to 10 cm, 4 in measured over Fair Isle pattern (tension dial setting approximately 7).
For perfect results, your tension must be matched exactly before starting the garment.

ABBREVIATIONS
See page 9.

NOTES
Knit side of knitting is right side of finished garment.
The card shown on page 00 should be punched, if required, before starting to knit. Two colour Fair Isle rows should be knitted with the first colour given in the back feeder 1(A) to knit the background and the second colour given in the front feeder 2(B) to knit the contrast pattern.

Linear summer top compliments the Zigzag patterned man's pullover.

FAIR ISLE PATTERN
K 2 rows MC/A, 6 rows A/B and 7 rows MC/B. These 15 rows form pattern.

BACK
Machines with ribber
With ribber in position and carriage at right, set machine for 1×1 rib. Push 69 [77, 84] Ns at left and right of centre 0 to WP. 138 [154, 168] Ns.
* Push corresponding Ns on ribber to WP. Arrange Ns for 1×1 rib. Using MC, cast on and K 3 tubular rows. Carriage is at right. Set carriage for 1×1 rib knitting. Set RC at 000. Using MT-5/MT-5, K 12 rows. Transfer sts for st st *.
Machines without ribber
Push 69 [76, 84] Ns at left and 68 [76, 83] Ns at right of centre 0 to WP. 137 [152, 167] Ns.
* Push every 3rd N back to NWP. Using MT and WY, cast on and K a few rows ending with carriage at left. Set RC at 000. Using MT-2 and MC, K 23 rows. Push Ns from NWP to WP and make a hem by placing loops of first row worked in MC evenly along the row. Unravel WY when work is completed *.
1st and 3rd sizes Inc 1 st at right edge.
2nd size Inc 1 st at both edges.
All sizes 138 [154, 168] sts.
All machines
Insert punchcard and lock on first row. Set carriage for patt. Set RC at 000. Using MT, K 1 row. Release card and cont in Fair Isle patt. K 3 rows. Shape sides by inc 1 st at each end of next and every foll 10th row until there are 156 [172, 186] sts. K 6 rows. RC shows 91 and work measures 26.5 cm, 10½ in.
Shape armholes Cast off (bind off) 5 sts at beg of next 2 rows. Dec 1 st at each end of next and every foll alt row until 114 [130, 144] sts rem **.
K 68 rows.
Shape neck Note patt row on card. Using a length of MC, cast off (bind off) centre 62 sts. Using nylon cord, K 26 [34, 41] sts at left by hand taking Ns down to NWP. Cont on rem sts for first side.
K 1 row. Dec 1 st at beg of next and foll alt row. 24 [32, 39] sts. Cont in st st. Using MC, K 2 rows. Using WY, K a few rows and release from machine.
With carriage at right, unravel nylon cord over rem Ns bringing Ns back to WP. Lock

card on number previously noted. Take carriage to left without knitting. Release card and cont in Fair Isle patt. Finish to correspond with first side.

FRONT
Work as for back to **.
K 44 rows.
Shape neck Note patt row on card. Using a length of MC, cast off (bind off) centre 42 sts. Using nylon cord, K 36 [44, 51] sts at left by hand taking Ns down to NWP. Cont on rem sts for first side.
K 1 row. Dec 1 st at beg of next and every foll alt row until 24 [32, 39] sts rem. K 4 rows. Cont in st st. Using MC, K 2 rows. Using WY, K a few rows and release from machine.
With carriage at right, unravel nylon cord over rem Ns bringing Ns back to WP. Lock card on number previously noted. Take

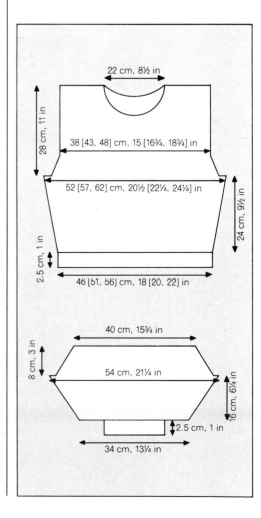

carriage to left without knitting. Release card and cont in Fair Isle patt. Finish to correspond with first side.

SLEEVES

Push 51 Ns at left and right of centre 0 to WP. 102 Ns. Using MT and WY, cast on and K a few rows ending with carriage at left. Insert punchcard and lock on first row. Set carriage for patt. Set RC at 000. Using MC, K 1 row. Release card and cont in Fair Isle patt. Shape sides by inc 1 st at each end of next and every foll alt row until there are 162 sts. K 1 row. RC shows 61 and work measures 16 cm, 6¼ in.

Shape top Cast off (bind off) 5 sts at beg of next 2 rows. Dec 1 st at each end of next and every foll alt row until 122 sts rem. Cont

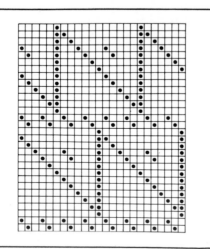

in st st. Using MC, dec 1 st at each end of next row. Cast off (bind off) rem 120 sts.

CUFFS

Machines with ribber

With ribber in position and carriage at right, set machine for 1×1 rib. Push 82 Ns to WP. Work as for back from * to *.

Machines without ribber

Push 80 Ns to WP. Work as for back from * to *.

All machines

With P side facing, replace 102 sts from lower edge of sleeve on to Ns gathering evenly. Using MT and MC, K 1 row. Cast off (bind off).

JOIN RIGHT SHOULDER

Push 24 [32, 39] Ns to WP. With K side of right back shoulder facing, replace sts on to Ns. With P side of right front shoulder facing, replace sts on to same Ns. Unravel WY. Using MT and MC, K 1 row. Cast off (bind off).

NECKBAND

Machines with ribber

With ribber in position and carriage at right, set machine for 1×1 rib. Using MC, cast on 150 sts in 1×1 rib. K 3 tubular rows. Carriage is at right. Set carriage for 1×1 rib knitting. Set RC at 000. Using MT-5/MT-5, K 24 rows. Transfer sts for st st. Using WY, K a few rows and release from machine.

Machines without ribber

Push 152 Ns to WP. With K side facing, pick

Short sleeved and 100% cotton, Linear summer top compliments the Zigzag patterned man's pullover.

up 152 sts around neck edge and place on to Ns. Using MT and MC, K 1 row. Transfer every 3rd st on to adjacent N and push empty Ns to NWP. Using MT-1, K 5 rows. Using MT-2, K 11 rows. Using MT-1, K 4 rows. Push Ns from NWP to WP and place loop from row below adjacent st on to empty Ns. Using MT, K 2 rows. Using WY, K a few rows and release from machine.

JOIN LEFT SHOULDER

Work as for right shoulder, reading left for right.

PRESSING

With wrong side facing, pin out all pieces to measurements given. Press carefully following instructions on cone band.

MAKING UP

Join side and sleeve seams. Set in sleeves. Join neckband seam.

Machines with ribber

Pin neckband into position. Unravelling WY as required, backstitch through open loops of last row worked in MC. Fold in half to inside and slipstitch down.

Machines without ribber

Fold neckband in half to right side and pin in position. Unravelling WY as required, backstitch through open loops of last row worked in MC.

Zigzag

The Classic Fair Isle pullover given a new look. Knit it
in cotton, or in warmer woollen colours for winter.

PATTERN RATING
● ● ● For fairly experienced knitters.

MACHINES
This pattern is suitable for standard gauge
punchcard machines.

MATERIALS
Rowan Cabled Mercerised Cotton.
210 [240, 270] g (8 [9, 10] oz) in shade 301
(MC).
150 [170, 190] g (5½ [6, 7] oz) in shade 304
(A).
120 [140, 160] g (4½ [5, 6] oz) in shade 310
(B).
50 [70, 90] g (2 [2½, 3] oz) in shade 315 (C).
50 [70, 90] g (2 [2½, 3] oz) in shade 308 (D).
*Rowan Cabled Mercerised Cotton is 100%
Pure Cotton.*

YARN THICKNESS
Medium yarn.

MEASUREMENTS
To fit chest 92-97 [102-107, 112-117] cm, 36-38
[40-42, 44-46] in.
Actual measurement 106 [116, 126] cm, 41¾
[45¾, 49½] in.
Length to shoulder 63.5 [65.5, 67.5] cm, 25
[25¾, 26½] in.
*Instructions are written for the smallest size,
larger sizes follow in square brackets. If only
one figure is given, it applies to all sizes.*

TENSION
31 stitches and 38 rows to 10 cm, 4 in
measured over Fair Isle pattern (tension dial
setting approximately 7).
*For perfect results, your tension must be
matched exactly before starting the
garment.*

ABBREVIATIONS
See page 9.

NOTES
Knit side of knitting is right side of finished
garment.
The card shown on page 22 should be
punched, if required, before starting to knit.
Two colour Fair Isle rows should be knitted
with the first colour given in the back feeder
1(A) to knit the background and the second
colour given in the front feeder 2(B) to knit
the contrast pattern.

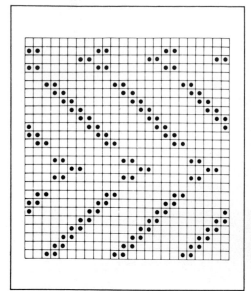

22

FAIR ISLE PATTERN

K 1 row MC/B, 6 rows A/B, 1 row MC/B, 1 row MC only (st st), 3 rows MC/C, 1 row MC only (st st), 1 row MC/B, 6 rows A/B, 1 row MC/B, 1 row MC only (st st), 3 rows MC/D and 1 row MC only (st st). These 26 rows form 1 pattern.

BACK

Machines with ribber

With ribber in position and carriage at right, set machine for 1×1 rib. Push 77 [85, 93] Ns at left and right of centre 0 to WP. 154 [170, 186] Ns. Push corresponding Ns on ribber to WP. Arrange Ns for 1×1 rib. Using MC, cast on and K 3 tubular rows. Carriage is at right. Set carriage for 1×1 rib knitting. Set RC at 000. Using MT-5/MT-5, K 20 rows. Transfer sts for st st.

Machines without ribber

Push 76 [85, 93] Ns at left and 76 [85, 92] Ns at right of centre 0 to WP. 152 [170, 185] Ns. Push every 3rd N back to NWP. Using MT and WY, cast on and K a few rows ending

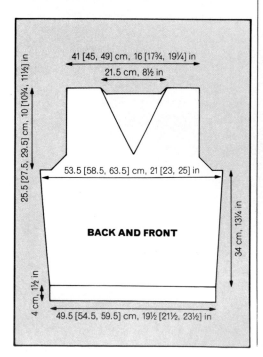

41 [45, 49] cm, 16 [17¾, 19¼] in

21.5 cm, 8½ in

25.5 [27.5, 29.5] cm, 10 [10¾, 11½] in

53.5 [58.5, 63.5] cm, 21 [23, 25] in

BACK AND FRONT

34 cm, 13¼ in

4 cm, 1½ in

49.5 [54.5, 59.5] cm, 19½ [21½, 23½] in

with carriage at left. Set RC at 000. Using MT-2 and MC, K 37 rows. Push Ns from NWP to WP and make a hem by placing loops of first row worked in MC evenly along the row. Unravel WY when work is completed.

1st size Inc 1 st at each end.
3rd size Inc 1 st at right edge.
All sizes 154 [170, 186] sts.
All machines
Insert punchcard and lock on first row. Set carriage for patt. Set RC at 000. Using MT, K 1 row. Release card and cont in Fair Isle patt. K 18 rows. Shape sides by inc 1 st at each end of next and every foll 20th row until there are 166 [182, 198] sts. K 10 rows. RC shows 130 and work measures 38 cm, 15 in.
Shape armholes Cast off (bind off) 10 sts at beg of next 2 rows. Dec 1 st at each end of every foll alt row until 128 [140, 152] sts rem. *. K 70 [74, 78] rows.
Shape back neck Note patt row on card. Using a length of MC, cast off (bind off) centre 64 sts. Using nylon cord, K 32 [38, 44] sts at left by hand taking Ns down to NWP. Cont on rem sts for first side.
K 1 row. Dec 1 st at beg of next and foll alt row. 30 [36, 42] sts. K 2 rows. Cont in st st. Using A [MC, A], K 1 row. Using WY, K a few rows and release from machine.
With carriage at right, unravel nylon cord over rem Ns bringing Ns back to WP. Lock card on number previously noted. Set carriage for patt and take to left without knitting. Release card and cont in Fair Isle patt. Finish to correspond with first side reversing shapings.

FRONT

Work as for back to *.
K 6 [10, 14] rows.
Shape neck Note patt row on card. Using nylon cord, K 64 [70, 76] sts at left by hand taking Ns down to NWP. Cont on rem sts for first side.
K 1 row. Dec 1 st at beg of next and every foll alt row until 30 [36, 42] sts rem. K 2 rows. Cont in st st. Using A [MC, A], K 1 row. Using WY, K a few rows and release from machine.
With carriage at right, unravel nylon cord over rem Ns bringing Ns back to WP. Lock card on number previously noted. Set carriage for patt and take to the left without knitting. Release card and cont in Fair Isle patt. Finish to correspond with first side reversing shapings.

TO JOIN RIGHT SHOULDER

Push 30 [36, 42] Ns to WP. With K side of right back shoulder facing, replace sts on to Ns. With P side of right front shoulder facing, replace sts on to same Ns. Unravel WY. Using MT and A [MC, A], K 1 row. Cast off (bind off).

TO JOIN LEFT SHOULDER

Work as for right shoulder reading left for right.

NECKBAND

Machines with ribber

With ribber in position and carriage at right, set machine for 1×1 rib. Using MC, cast on 195 sts in 1×1 rib.
* K 3 tubular rows. Carriage is at right. Set carriage for 1×1 rib knitting. Set RC at 000. Using MT-5/MT-5, K 24 rows. Transfer sts for st st. Using WY, K a few rows and release from machine *.

Machines without ribber

Push 197 Ns to WP.
* Push every 3rd N back to NWP. Using MT and WY, cast on and K a few rows ending with carriage at left. Set RC at 000. Using MT-1 and MC, K 5 rows. Using MT-2, K 13 rows. Using MT-1, K 5 rows. Push Ns from NWP to WP and make a hem by placing loops of first row worked in MC evenly along the row. Unravel WY when work is completed. Using MT, K 2 rows. Using WY, K a few rows and release from machine *.

ARMHOLE BAND

Machines with ribber

With ribber in position and carriage at right, set machine for 1×1 rib. Using MC, cast on 165 [181, 197] sts in 1×1 rib. Work as for neckband from * to *.

Machines without ribber

Push 167 [182, 197] Ns to WP. Work as for neckband from * to *.

PRESSING

With wrong side facing, pin out all pieces to measurements given. Press carefully following instructions on cone band.

MAKING UP

Pin neckband and armhole bands into position. Unravelling WY as required, backstitch through open loops of last row worked in MC. Join side and armhole band seams.

Machines with ribber

Fold neckband and armhole bands in half to inside and slipstich down.

All machines

Cross ends of neckband left over right and slipstitch down.

Child's Zigzag

A pretty sweater using the same pattern as the pullover. For a boy, simply change the colours.

PATTERN RATING
● ● ● For fairly experienced knitters.

MACHINES
This pattern is suitable for standard gauge punchcard machines.

MATERIALS
Rowan Cabled Mercerised Cotton.
145 [155, 165, 175] g (5 [5½, 6, 6½] oz) in shade 301 (MC).
120 [130, 140, 150] g (4½ [5, 5, 5½] oz) in shade 312 (A).
90 [100, 110, 120] g (3½ [4, 4, 4½] oz) in shade 316 (B).
35 [40, 45, 50] g (1½ [1½, 2, 2] oz) in shade 323 (C).
35 [40, 45, 50] g (1½ [1½, 2, 2] oz) in shade 308 (D).
Rowan Cabled Mercerised Cotton is 100% Pure Cotton.

YARN THICKNESS
Medium yarn.

MEASUREMENTS
To fit chest 61 [66, 71, 76] cm, 24 [26, 28, 30] in.
Actual measurement 67 [72, 77, 82] cm, 26½ [28¼, 30¼, 32¼] in.
Length to shoulder 37.5 [40.5, 43.5, 46.5] cm, 14¾ [16, 17, 18¼] in.
Sleeve seam 28 [31, 34, 37] cm, 11 [12¼, 13½, 14½] in.
Instructions are written for the smallest size, larger sizes follow in square brackets. If only one figure is given, it applies to all sizes.

TENSION
31 stitches and 38 rows to 10 cm, 4 in measured over Fair Isle pattern (tension dial setting approximately 7).
For perfect results, your tension must be matched exactly before starting the garment.

ABBREVIATIONS
See page 9.

NOTES
Knit side of knitting is right side of finished garment.
The card shown on page 22 should be punched, if required, before starting to knit.
Two colour Fair Isle rows should be knitted

with the first colour given in the back feeder 1(A) to knit the background and the second colour given in the front feeder 2(B) to knit the contrast pattern.

FAIR ISLE PATTERN

K 1 row MC/B, 6 rows A/B, 1 row MC/B, 1 row MC only (st st), 3 rows MC/C, 1 row MC only (st st), 1 row MC/B, 6 rows A/B, 1 row MC/B, 1 row MC only (st st), 3 rows MC/D and 1 row MC only (st st). These 26 rows form 1 pattern.

BACK
Machines with ribber

With ribber in position and carriage at right, set machine for 1×1 rib. Push 44 [48, 52, 56] Ns at left and right of centre 0 to WP. 88 [96, 104, 112] Ns.
* Push corresponding Ns on ribber to WP. Arrange Ns for 1×1 rib. Using MC, cast on and K 3 tubular rows. Carriage is at right.
Set carriage for 1×1 rib knitting.
Set RC at 000.
Using MT-5/MT-5, K 20 rows.

Transfer sts for st st *.
Machines without ribber

Push 43 [48, 52, 55] Ns at left and 43 [47, 52, 55] Ns at right of centre 0 to WP. 86 [95, 104, 110] Ns.
* Push every 3rd N back to NWP.
Using MT and WY, cast on and K a few rows ending with carriage at left.
Set RC at 000. Using MT-2 and MC, K 37 rows.
Push Ns from NWP to WP and make a hem by placing loops of first row worked in MC

evenly along the row. Unravel WY when work is completed *.
1st and 4th sizes Inc 1 st at each end.
2nd size Inc 1 st at right edge.
All sizes 88 [96, 104, 112] sts.
All machines
Insert punchcard and lock on first row. Set carriage for patt. Set RC at 000. Using MT, K 1 row. Release card and cont in Fair Isle patt. K 6 rows. Shape sides by inc 1 st at each end of next and every foll 5th [6th, 7th, 8th] row until there are 106 [114, 122, 130] sts. K 10 [10, 10, 8] rows. RC shows 58 [66, 74, 80] and work measures 19 [21, 23, 25] cm, 7½ [8¼, 9, 9¾] in.
Shape armholes Cast off (bind off) 11 [11, 12, 12] sts at beg of next 2 rows. 84 [92, 98, 106] sts **.
K 62 [66, 70, 74] rows.
Shape neck Note patt row on card. Using a length of A [A, A, MC] cast off (bind off) centre 44 [46, 48, 50] sts.
Using nylon cord, K 20 [23, 25, 28] sts at left by hand taking Ns down to NWP. Cont on rem sts for first side.
K 1 row. Dec 1 st at beg of next and foll alt row. 18 [21, 23, 26] sts. K 1 row. Cont in st st. Using MC [MC, MC, A], K 1 row. Using WY, K a few rows and release from machine. With carriage at right, unravel nylon cord over rem Ns bringing Ns back to WP. Lock card on number previously noted. Take carriage to left without knitting. Release card and cont in Fair Isle patt. Finish to correspond with first side.

FRONT
Work as for back to **.
K 41 [45, 45, 49] rows.
Shape neck Note patt row on card. Using a length of MC [MC, A, MC], cast off (bind off) centre 24 [26, 28, 30] sts. Using nylon cord, K 30 [33, 35, 38] sts at right by hand taking Ns down to NWP. Cont on rem sts for first side.
K 1 row. Dec 1 st at beg of next and every foll alt row until 18 [21, 23, 26] sts rem. K 2 [2, 6, 6] rows. Cont in st st. Using MC [MC, MC, A], K 1 row. Using WY, K a few rows and release from machine.
With carriage at left, unravel nylon cord over rem Ns bringing Ns back to WP. Lock card on number previously noted. Take carriage to right without knitting. Release card and cont in Fair Isle patt. Finish to correspond with first side.

SLEEVES
Machines with ribber
With ribber in position and carriage at right, set machine for 1×1 rib. Push 27 [27, 28, 28] Ns at left and right of centre 0 to WP. 54 [54, 56, 56] Ns. Work as for back from * to *.
Machines without ribber
Push 27 [27, 28, 28] Ns at left and 26 [26, 28, 28] Ns at right of centre 0 to WP. 53 [53, 56, 56] Ns. Work as for back from * to *.
1st and 2nd sizes Inc 1 st at right edge.
All sizes 54 [54, 56, 56] sts.

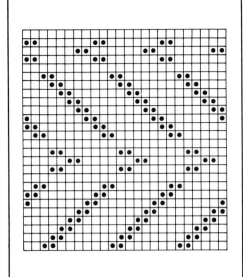

All machines
Insert punchcard and lock on first row. Set carriage for patt. Set RC at 000. Using MT, K 1 row. Release card and cont in Fair Isle patt. Shape sides by inc 1 st at each end of next and every foll 3rd row until there are 116 [122, 128, 134] sts. K 0 [3, 7, 10] rows. RC shows 92 [104, 114, 126] and work measures 28 [31, 34, 37] cm, 11 [12¼, 13½, 14½] in. Place marker at each end. K 13 [13, 14, 14] rows. Cont in st st. Using MC, K 1 row. Using WY, K a few rows and release from machine.

TO JOIN RIGHT SHOULDER
Push 18 [21, 23, 26] Ns to WP. With K side of right back shoulder facing, replace sts on to Ns. With P side of right front shoulder facing, replace sts on to same Ns. Unravel WY. Using MT and MC [MC, MC, A], K 1 row. Cast off (bind off).

NECKBAND
Machines with ribber
With ribber in position and carriage at right, set machine for 1×1 rib. Using MC, cast on 128 [132, 136, 140] sts in 1×1 rib. K 3 tubular rows. Carriage is at right. Set carriage for

1×1 rib knitting. Set RC at 000. Using MT-5/MT-5, K 24 rows. Transfer sts for st st. Using WY, K a few rows and release from machine.
Machines without ribber
Push 128 [131, 137, 140] Ns to WP. With K side facing, pick up 128 [131, 137, 140] sts around neck edge and place on to Ns. Using MT and MC, K 1 row. Transfer every 3rd st on to adjacent N and push empty Ns to NWP. Using MT-1, K 5 rows. Using MT-2, K 11 rows. Using MT-1, K 4 rows. Push Ns from NWP to WP and place loop from row below adjacent st on to empty Ns. Using MT, K 2 rows. Using WY, K a few rows and release from machine.

TO JOIN LEFT SHOULDER
Work as for right shoulder reading left for right.

JOIN SLEEVES TO ARMHOLES
Push 116 [122, 128, 134] Ns to WP. With K side of sleeve facing, replace 116 [122, 128, 134] sts on to Ns. With P side of armhole facing, pick up 116 [122, 128, 134] sts along side edge and place on to same Ns. Unravel WY. Using MT and MC, K 1 row. Cast off (bind off).

PRESSING
With wrong side facing, pin out all pieces to measurements given. Press carefully following instructions on cone band.

MAKING UP
Sew rows above markers on sleeves to cast off (bound off) sts on back and front. Join side and sleeve seams. Join neckband seam.
Machines with ribber
Pin neckband into position. Unravelling WY as required, backstitch through open loops of last row worked in MC. Fold in half to inside and slipstitch down.
Machines without ribber
Fold neckband in half to right side and pin in position. Unravelling WY as required, backstitch through open loops of last row worked in MC.

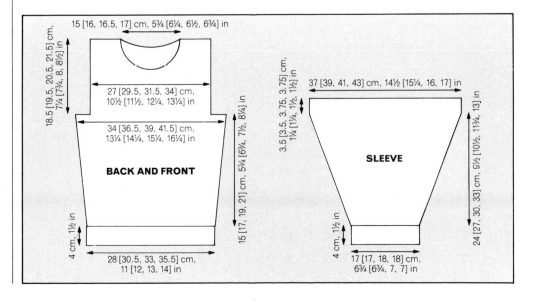

Domino

This cropped sweater tapers slightly at the
waist, with an unusual square neckline and wide sleeves
tapering down to the cuff.

26 PATTERN RATING
●● Fairly easy, for knitters with some
experience.

MACHINES
This pattern is suitable for standard gauge
punchcard machines.

MATERIALS
Rowan Cabled Mercerised Cotton.
350 [375, 400] g (13 [13½, 14] oz) in shade 301
(MC).
325 [350, 375] g (12 [13, 13½] oz) in shade
308 (C).
*Rowan Cabled Mercerised Cotton is 100%
Pure Cotton.*

YARN THICKNESS
Medium yarn.

MEASUREMENTS
To fit chest 76-82 [87-92, 97-102] cm, 30-32
[34-36, 38-40] in.
Actual measurement 101 [111, 121] cm, 39¾
[43¾, 47¾].
Length to shoulder 52.5 cm, 20¾ in.
Sleeve seam 48.5 cm, 19 in.
*Instructions are written for the smallest size,
larger sizes follow in square brackets. If only
one figure is given, it applies to all sizes.*

TENSION
30 stitches and 38 rows to 10 cm, 4 in

measured over Fair Isle pattern (tension dial
setting approximately 7).
*For perfect results, your tension must be
matched exactly before starting the
garment.*

ABBREVIATIONS
See page 9.

NOTES
Knit side of knitting is right side of finished
garment.
The card shown on page 28 should be
punched, if required, before starting to knit.

BACK
Machines with ribber
With ribber in position and carriage at right,
set machine for 1×1 rib. Push 58 [65, 73] Ns
at left and right of centre 0 to WP. 116 [130,
146] Ns.
* Push corresponding Ns on ribber to WP.
Arrange Ns for 1×1 rib. Using MC, cast on
and K 3 tubular rows. Carriage is at right.
Set carriage for 1×1 rib knitting. Set RC at
000. Using MT-5/MT-5, K 20 rows. Transfer
sts for st st *.
Machines without ribber
Push 58 [64, 73] Ns at left and right of centre
O to WP. 116 [128, 146] Ns.
* Push every 3rd N back to NWP. Using MT
and WY, cast on and K a few rows ending
with carriage at left. Set RC at 000. Using

MT-2 and MC, K 37 rows. Push Ns from
NWP to WP and make a hem by placing
loops of first row worked in MC evenly along
the row. Unravel WY when work is
completed *.
2nd size Inc 1 st at each end.
All sizes 116 [130, 146] sts.
All machines
Insert punchcard and lock on first row. Set
carriage for patt. Set RC at 000. Using MT, K
1 row. Release card and cont in Fair Isle patt
with MC in feeder 1(A) and C in feeder 2(B).
K 2 rows. Shape sides by inc 1 st at each
end of next and every foll 4th row until there
are 154 [168, 184] sts. K 10 rows. RC shows
86 and work measures 26.5 cm, 10½ in.
Shape armholes Cast off (bind off) 23 sts
at beg of next row and 22 sts at beg of foll
row. 109 [123, 139] sts **.
K 82 rows.
Shape neck Note patt row on card. Using a
length of MC, cast off centre (bind off) 69
sts. Using nylon cord, K 20 [27, 35] sts at left
by hand taking Ns down to NWP. Cont on
rem sts for first side.
K 14 rows. Cont in st st. Using MC, K 1 row.
Using WY, K a few rows and release from
machine.
With carriage at right, unravel nylon cord
over rem Ns bringing Ns back to WP. Lock
card on number previously noted. Take
carriage to left without knitting. Release
card and cont in Fair Isle patt. Finish to
correspond with first side.

FRONT
Work as for back to **.
K 68 rows.
Shape neck Note patt row on card. Using a
length of MC, cast off centre (bind off) 69
sts. Using nylon cord, K 20 [27, 35] sts at left
by hand taking Ns down to NWP. Cont on
rem sts for first side.
K 28 rows. Cont in st st. Using MC, K 1 row.
Using WY, K a few rows and release from
machine.
With carriage at right, unravel nylon cord
over rem Ns bringing Ns back to WP. Lock
card on number previously noted. Take

*A popular game is the inspiration for the
repeating pattern on the Domino sweater,
whereas a slightly abstract version of an
allover geometric design forms the
Diamond patterned jersey.*

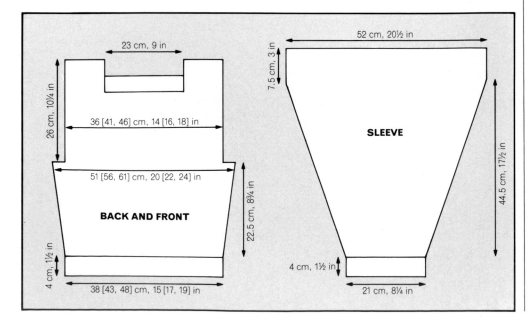

28

carriage to left without knitting. Release card and cont in Fair Isle patt. Finish to correspond with first side.

SLEEVES

Machines with ribber
With ribber in position and carriage at right, set machine for 1×1 rib. Push 31 Ns at left and right of centre 0 to WP. 62 Ns. Work as for back from * to *.

Machines without ribber
Push 31 Ns at left and right of centre 0 to WP. 62 Ns. Work as for back from * to *.

All machines
Inc 1 st at left edge. 63 sts. Insert punchcard and lock on first row. Set carriage for patt. Set RC at 000. Using MT, K 1 row. Release card and cont in Fair Isle patt with MC in feeder 1(A) and C in feeder 2(B), K 2 rows. Shape sides by inc 1 st at each end of next and every foll 3rd row until there are 157 sts. K 28 rows. RC shows 170 and work

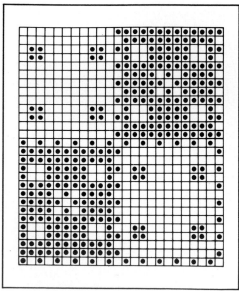

measures 48.5 cm, 19 in. Place a marker at each end. K 28 rows. Cont in st st. Using MC, K 1 row. Using WY, K a few rows and release from machine.

TO JOIN RIGHT SHOULDER
Push 20 [27, 35] Ns to WP. With K side of right back shoulder facing, replace sts on to Ns. With P side of right front shoulder facing, replace sts on to same Ns. Unravel WY. Using MT and MC, K 1 row. Cast off (bind off).

TO JOIN LEFT SHOULDER
Work as for right shoulder reading left for right.

BACK AND FRONT NECKBANDS
Machines with ribber
With ribber in position and carriage at right, set machine for 1×1 rib. Using MC, cast on 71 sts in 1×1 rib.
* K 3 tubular rows. Carriage is at right. Set carriage for 1×1 rib knitting. Set RC at 000. Using MT-5/MT-5, K 10 rows. Transfer sts for st st. Using WY, K a few rows and release from machine *.

Machines without ribber
Push 69 Ns to WP. With K side facing, pick up 69 sts across neck edge and place on to Ns, inc 1 st at each edge. 71 sts.
* Using MT and MC, K 1 row. Transfer every 3rd st on to adjacent N and push empty Ns to NWP. Using MT-2, K 16 rows. Push Ns from NWP to WP and place loop from row below adjacent st on to empty Ns. Using MT, K 2 rows. Using WY, K a few rows and release from machine *.

SIDE NECKBANDS
Machines with ribber
With ribber in position and carriage at right, set machine for 1×1 rib. Using MC, cast on 38 sts in 1×1 rib. Work as for back and front neckband from * to *.

Machines without ribber
Push 38 Ns to WP. With K side facing, pick up 38 sts along side edge of neck and place on to Ns. Work as for back and front neckband from * to *.

JOIN SLEEVES TO ARMHOLES
Push 157 Ns to WP. With K side of sleeve facing, replace 157 sts on to Ns. With P side of armhole facing, pick up 157 sts along side edge and place on to same Ns. Unravel WY. Using MT and MC, K 1 row. Cast off (bind off).

PRESSING
With wrong side facing, pin out all pieces to measurements given. Press carefully following instructions on cone band.

MAKING UP
Sew rows above markers on sleeves to cast off (bound off) sts on back and front. Join side and sleeve seams.

Machines with ribber
Pin neckbands into position. Unravelling WY as required, backstitch through open loops of last row worked in MC.

Machines without ribber
Fold neckbands in half to right side and pin in position. Unravelling WY as required, backstitch through open loops of last row worked in MC.

All machines
Lap front and back neckbands over side neckbands and slipstich down.

Diamonds

Knitted in cotton, with short sleeves and a band of
black diamonds above the body ribs and along the sleeve tops.

PATTERN RATING
●● Fairly easy, for knitters with some
experience.

MACHINES
This pattern is suitable for standard gauge
punchcard machines.

MATERIALS
Rowan Cabled Mercerised Cotton.
500 g (18 oz) in shade 301 (MC).
200 g (7 oz) in shade 318 (A).
50 g (2 oz) in shade 319 (B).
*Rowan Cabled Mercerised Cotton is 100%
Pure Cotton.*

YARN THICKNESS
Medium yarn.

MEASUREMENTS
To fit chest 87-97 cm, 34-38 in.
Actual measurement 112 cm, 44 in.
Length to shoulder 73.5 cm, 29 in.
Sleeve seam 19.5 cm, 7¾ in.

TENSION
29.5 stitches and 39 rows to 10 cm, 4 in.
measured over Fair Isle pattern (tension dial
setting approximately 7).
*For perfect results, your tension must be
matched exactly before starting the
garment.*

ABBREVIATIONS
See page 9.

NOTES
Knit side of knitting is right side of finished
garment.
The card shown on page 30 should be
punched, if required, before starting to knit.

BACK
Machines with ribber
With ribber in position and carriage at right,
set machine for 1×1 rib. Push 77 Ns at left
and right of centre 0 to WP. 154 Ns. Push
corresponding Ns on ribber to WP. Arrange
Ns for 1×1 rib. Using MC, cast on and K 3
tubular rows. Carriage is at right. Set
carriage for 1×1 rib knitting. Set RC at 000.
Using MT-5/MT-5, K 12 rows. Transfer sts for
st st.
Machines without ribber
Push 76 Ns at left and 76 Ns at right of

centre 0 to WP. 152 Ns.
* Push every 3rd N back to NWP. Using MT
and WY, cast on and K a few rows ending
with carriage at left. Set RC at 000. Using
MT-2 and MC, K 23 rows.
Push Ns from NWP to WP and make a hem
by placing loops of first row worked in MC
evenly along the row. Unravel WY when

work is completed *.
Inc 1 st at each end. 154 sts.
All machines
Insert punchcard and lock on first row. Set
carriage for patt. Set RC at 000. Using MT, K
1 row. Release card and cont in Fair Isle
patt, with MC in feeder 1(A) and B in feeder
2(B). K 23 rows. Shape sides by inc 1 st at

30

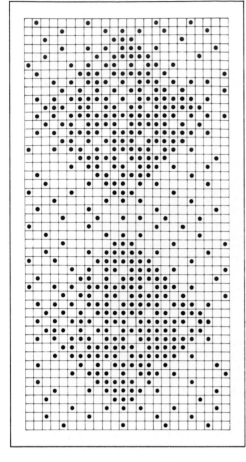

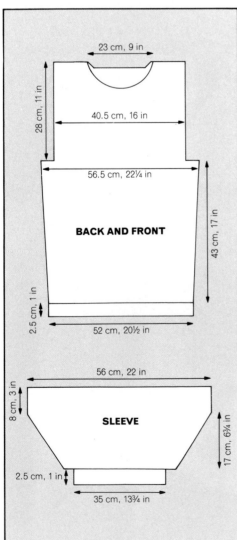

23 cm, 9 in

28 cm, 11 in

40.5 cm, 16 in

56.5 cm, 22¼ in

43 cm, 17 in

BACK AND FRONT

2.5 cm, 1 in

52 cm, 20½ in

56 cm, 22 in

8 cm, 3 in

SLEEVE

17 cm, 6¾ in

2.5 cm, 1 in

35 cm, 13¾ in

each end of next row. With MC in feeder 1(A) and A in feeder 2(B), cont to inc on every 24th row from previous inc until there are 168 sts. RC shows 169 and work measures 45.5 cm, 18 in.

Shape armholes Cast off (bind off) 24 sts at beg of next 2 rows. 120 sts **.
K 101 rows.

Shape back neck Note patt row on card. Using a length of MC, cast off (bind off) centre 64 sts. Using nylon cord, K 28 sts at left by hand taking Ns down to NWP. Cont on rem sts for first side.
K 1 row. Dec 1 st at beg of next and foll alt row. 26 sts. K 1 row. Cont in st st. Using MC, K 1 row. Using WY, K a few rows and release from machine.
With carriage at right, unravel nylon cord over rem Ns bringing Ns back to WP. Lock card on number previously noted. Set carriage for patt and take to left without knitting. Release card and cont in Fair Isle patt. Finish to correspond with first side reversing shapings.

FRONT

Work as for back to **.
K 71 rows.

Shape neck Note patt row on card. Using a length of MC, cast off (bind off) centre 36 sts. Using nylon cord, K 42 sts at left by hand taking Ns down to NWP. Cont on rem sts for first side.
K 1 row. Dec 1 st at beg of next and every foll alt row until 26 sts rem. K 3 rows. Cont in st st. Using MC, K 1 row. Using WY, K a few rows and release from machine.
With carriage at right, unravel nylon cord over rem Ns bringing Ns back to WP. Lock card on number previously noted. Set carriage for patt and take to left without knitting. Release card and cont in Fair Isle patt. Finish to correspond with first side reversing shapings.

SLEEVES

Push 52 Ns at left and right of centre 0 to WP. 104 Ns. Using MT and WY, cast on and K a few rows ending with carriage at right. Insert punchcard and lock on first row. Set carriage for patt. Set RC at 000. Using MC, K 1 row. Release card and cont in Fair Isle patt with MC in feeder 1(A) and A in feeder 2(B). Shape sides by inc 1 st at each end of next and every foll alt row until there are 166 sts. K 5 rows. RC shows 67 and work measures 17 cm, 6¾ in. Place marker at each end. K 6 rows. With MC in feeder 1(A) and B in feeder 2(B), K 24 rows. Cont in st st. Using MC, K 1 row. Using WY, K a few rows and release from machine.

CUFFS
Machines with ribber
With ribber in position and carriage at right, set machine for 1×1 rib. Using MC, cast on 84 sts in 1×1 rib. K 3 tubular rows. Carriage is at right. Set carriage for 1×1 rib knitting. Set RC at 000. Using MT-5/MT-5, K

12 rows. Transfer sts for st st.
Machines without ribber
Push 83 Ns to WP. Work as for back from * to *.
All machines
With P side of sleeve facing, replace sts on to Ns gathering evenly. Unravel WY. Using MT and MC, K 1 row. Cast off (bind off).

TO JOIN RIGHT SHOULDER
Push 26 Ns to WP. With K side of right back shoulder facing, replace sts on to Ns. With P side of right front shoulder facing, replace sts on to same Ns. Unravel WY. Using MT and MC, K 1 row. Cast off (bind off).

NECKBAND
Machines with ribber
With ribber in position and carriage at right, set machine for 1×1 rib. Using MC, cast on 160 sts in 1×1 rib. K 3 tubular rows. Carriage is at right. Set carriage for 1×1 rib knitting. Set RC at 000. Using MT-5/MT-5, K 24 rows. Transfer sts for st st. Using WY, K a few rows and release from machine.
Machines without ribber
Push 161 Ns to WP. With K side facing, pick up 161 sts around neck edge and place on to Ns. Using MT and MC, K 1 row. Transfer every 3rd st on to adjacent N and push empty Ns to NWP. Using MT-1, K 5 rows. Using MT-2, K 11 rows. Using MT-1, K 4 rows. Push Ns from NWP to WP and place loop from row below adjacent st on to empty Ns. Using MT, K 2 rows. Using WY, K a few rows and release from machine.

TO JOIN LEFT SHOULDER
Work as for right shoulder reading left for right.

TO JOIN SLEEVES TO ARMHOLES
Push 166 Ns to WP. With K side of sleeve facing, replace 166 sts on to Ns. With P side of armhole facing, pick up 166 sts along side edge and place on to same Ns. Unravel WY. Using MT and MC, K 1 row. Cast off (bind off).

PRESSING
With wrong side facing, pin out all pieces to measurements given. Press carefully following instructions on cone band.

MAKING UP
Sew rows above markers on sleeves to cast off (bound off) sts on back and front. Join side, sleeve and neckband seams.
Machines with ribber
Pin neckband into position. Unravelling WY as required, backstitch through open loops of last row worked in MC. Fold in half to inside and slipstitch down.
Machines without ribber
Fold neckband in half to right side and pin in position.
Unravelling WY as required backstitch through the open loops of the last row worked in MC.

Transatlantic

In choosing the title Transatlantic I tried to suggest the filtration of the Fifties American popular youth culture into British society, when films such as *Rebel Without A Cause, Blackboard Jungle* and *The Wild Ones* defined the age. The style and the American myth are still very strong in contemporary culture, on both sides of the Atlantic.

It's impossible to ignore, then, the ubiquitous baseball jacket. The Baseball cardigan design has obvious references to this, with striped knitted ribs and contrasting marled grey sleeves. The inset collar fits neatly onto the right angle formed by the side front panels and front button ribs, and the two pockets make it a practical classic.

The Babe Ruth design, named after the famous baseball player, also derived from the baseball jacket. It has contrasting ribs and sleeves, and two deep pockets with a simple crew neck. This two-toned cardigan is knitted with a marled grey and solid black yarn, but alternative combinations such as black and dark red would also work. The skirt is simple to make and obviously practical if worn without the cardigan. The length can be altered by omitting or adding rows.

In 1953 the Cadillac Eldorado had arrived; the bigger tail fins were a mere hint of things to come. The Fifties consumer extravaganza was at its height and, excluding ecological considerations, these cars with their sculptured panels and chrome bumpers were beautiful and very expressive products of industrial design.

The American truck also has all the associations of cult romance. The individual customization of these enormous trucks is both ingenious and fascinating. Trucking or Eldorado would make very special sweaters for a child, boy or girl, and the graphs can be used in conjunction with an adult's basic pattern if there are some older enthusiasts around! They do take quite a lot of patience but the enthusiasm shown for their sweaters by Jamie and Tommy, the two boys in the photographs, makes the effort worthwhile.

The New Jersey sweater is a classic in the American sportswear tradition. In cotton or wool, it is a very practical sweater. There are two versions shown: one has a crew neck, the other a collar. The stripe at the top of the sleeve fits squarely into the front and back armhole inset, the depth of which corresponds to the width of the stripe. Ignoring this consideration, the stripe width could be made finer or thicker.

All the sweaters in Transatlantic are easy to knit, although I would recommend tackling the intarsia sweaters – Eldorado and Trucking – only if you are already familiar with the intarsia technique. Dividing sweaters into areas or blocks of colour or stripes can be extended into a variety of design themes.

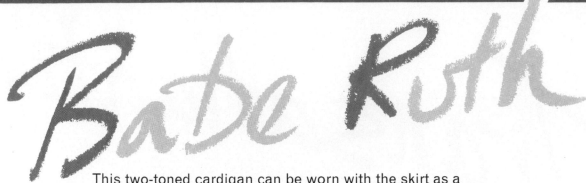

Babe Ruth

This two-toned cardigan can be worn with the skirt as a
suit or on its own. It has two practical pockets, contrasting sleeves and ribs.

32 PATTERN RATING
● Easy to knit.

MACHINES
This pattern is suitable for standard gauge
machines.

MATERIALS
Brockwell's Lambswool 3 ply (scoured).
275 [300, 325] g (10 [11, 12] oz) in Black (MC).
240 [255, 270] g (8½ [9, 9½] oz) in Light Grey
Grey (C).
6 buttons.
*Brockwell's Lambswool 3 ply is 100% Pure
Lambswool.*

YARN THICKNESS
Medium fine yarn.

MEASUREMENTS
To fit chest 76-82 [87-92, 97-102] cm, 30-32
[34-36, 38-40] in.
Actual measurement 109 [119, 129] cm, 43
[46¾, 50¾] in.
Length to shoulder 76.5 cm, 30¼ in.
Sleeve seam 45.5 cm, 18 in.
*Instructions are written for the smallest size,
larger sizes follow in square brackets. If only
one figure is given, it applies to all sizes.*

TENSION
26 stitches and 41 rows to 10 cm, 4 in
measured over stocking stitch (tension dial
setting approximately 7).
*For perfect results, your tension must be
matched exactly before starting the
garment.*

ABBREVIATIONS
See page 9.

NOTES
Knit side of knitting is right side of finished
garment.

BACK
Machines with ribber
With ribber in position and carriage at right,
set machine for 1×1 rib. Using C, cast on
132 [144, 158] sts in 1×1 rib.
* K 3 tubular rows. Carriage is at right. Set
carriage for 1×1 rib knitting. Set RC at 000.
Using MT-7/MT-7, K 10 rows. Transfer sts for
st st *.
Machines without ribber
Push 131 [143, 158] Ns to WP.
* Push every 3rd N back to NWP. Using MT
and WY, cast on and K a few rows ending
with carriage at left. Set RC at 000. Using
MT-4 and C, K 19 rows. Push Ns from NWP
to WP and make a hem by placing loops of
first row worked in C evenly along the row.
Unravel WY when work is completed *.
1st and 2nd sizes Inc 1 st.

All sizes 132 [144, 158] sts.
All machines
Set RC at 000. Using MT and MC, K 19
rows. Shape sides by inc 1 st at each end of
next and every foll 20th row until there are
144 [156, 170] sts. K 62 rows. RC shows 182
and work measures 46.5 cm, 18¼ in.
Shape armholes Cast off (bind off) 23 sts
at beg of next 2 rows. 98 [110, 124] sts. K 116
rows.
Shape neck Using a length of MC, cast off
(bind off) centre 46 sts. Push 26 [32, 39] Ns
at left to HP and cont on rem sts for first
side.
K 1 row. Dec 1 st at beg of next and foll alt
row. 24 [30, 37] sts. K 2 rows. Using WY, K
a few rows and release from machine.
With carriage at left, push rem Ns from HP
to UWP and finish to correspond with first
side reversing shapings.

RIGHT FRONT
Machines with ribber
With ribber in position and carriage at right,
set machine for 1×1 rib. Using C, cast on 64
[70, 77] sts in 1×1 rib. Work as for back from
* to *.
Machines without ribber
Push 62 [68, 77] Ns to WP. Work as for back
from * to *.
1st and 2nd sizes Inc 1 st at each end.
All sizes 64 [70, 77] sts.
All machines
Set RC at 000. Using MT and MC, K 19
rows. Shape side by inc 1 st at right edge
(left edge on left front) of next and every foll
20th row until there are 70 [76, 83] sts. K 62
rows. RC shows 182 and work measures
46.5 cm, 18¼ in. K 1 row extra for left front
only.
Shape armhole Cast off (bind off) 23 sts at
beg of next row. 47 [53, 60] sts. K 94 rows.
Shape neck Cast off (bind off) 10 sts at beg
of next row. Dec 1 st (2 sts in) at neck edge
on every row until 24 [30, 37] sts rem. K 15
rows. Using WY, K a few rows and release
from machine.

LEFT FRONT
Work as for right front reversing shapings by
noting alteration in number of rows worked.

*The man's Baseball cardigan, shown here
with Babe Ruth cardigan and skirt, show
alternative colours for making this suit.*

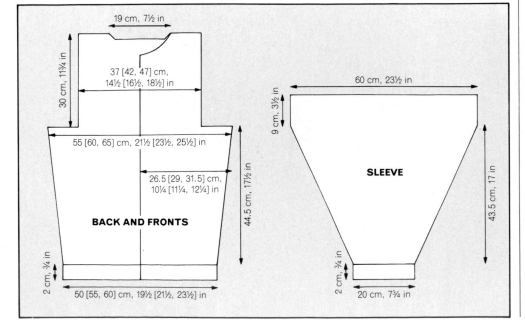

SLEEVES
Machines with ribber
With ribber in position and carriage at right, set machine for 1×1 rib. Using MC, cast on 52 sts in 1×1 rib. Work as for back from * to *.
Machines without ribber
Push 50 Ns to WP. Push every 3rd N back to NWP. Using MT and WY, cast on and K a few rows ending with carriage at left. Set RC at 000. Using MT-4 and MC, K 19 rows. Push Ns from NWP to WP and make a hem by placing loops of first row worked in MC evenly along the row. Unravel WY when work is completed. Inc 1 st at each end. 52 sts.
All machines
Set RC at 000. Using MT and C, K 2 rows. Shape sides by inc 1 st (2 sts in) at each end of next and every foll 3rd row until there are 156 sts. K 23 rows. RC shows 179 and work measures 45.5 cm, 18 in. Place marker at each end. K 37 rows. Using WY, K a few rows and release from machine.

POCKETS
Push 38 Ns to WP. Using MT and WY, cast on and K a few rows ending with carriage at left. Set RC at 000. Using MC, K 58 rows. Using WY, K a few rows and release from machine.

POCKET TOPS
Machines with ribber
With ribber in position and carriage at right, set machine for 1×1 rib. Using C, cast on 38 sts in 1×1 rib. Work as for back from * to *.
Machines without ribber
Push 38 Ns to WP. Work as for back from * to *.
All machines
With P side facing, replace sts from top of pocket on to Ns. Using MT and MC, K 1 row. Cast off (bind off).

BUTTONHOLE BAND
Machines with ribber
With ribber in position and carriage at right, set machine for 1×1 rib. Using MC, cast on 193 sts in 1×1 rib. K 3 tubular rows. Carriage is at right. Set carriage for 1×1 rib knitting. Set RC at 000. Using MT-6/MT-6, K 6 rows. Counting from left edge, make buttonholes over Ns 7, 8; 43, 44; 79, 80; 115, 116; 151, 152; 187 and 188. K 15 rows. Make buttonholes over same Ns as before. K 6 rows. Transfer sts for st st. Using WY, K a few rows and release from machine. Pin into position. Unravelling WY as required, backstitch through open loops of last row worked in MC. Fold in half to inside and slipstich down.
Machines without ribber
Push 181 Ns to WP. With K side facing, pick up 181 sts along right front edge and place on to Ns. Set RC at 000. Using MT-1 and MC, K 5 rows. Counting from left edge, make buttonholes over Ns 6, 7; 40, 41; 74, 75; 108, 109; 142, 143; 176 and 177. K 11 rows. Make buttonholes over same Ns as before.

K 5 rows. Transfer sts for st st. Using WY, K a few rows and release from machine. Fold in half to right side and pin into position. Unravelling WY as required, backstitch through open loops of last row worked in MC.

BUTTON BAND
Machines with ribber
Work as for buttonhole band omitting buttonholes.
Machines without ribber
Work as for buttonhole band omitting buttonholes and read left for right.

TO JOIN RIGHT SHOULDER
Push 24 [30, 37] Ns to WP. With K side of right back shoulder facing, replace sts on to Ns. With P side of right front shoulder facing, replace sts on to same Ns. Using MT and MC, K 1 row. Cast off (bind off).

TO JOIN LEFT SHOULDER
Work as for right shoulder but read left for right.

NECKBAND
Machines with ribber
With ribber in position and carriage at right, set machine for 1×1 rib. Using C, cast on 150 sts in 1×1 rib. K 3 tubular rows. Carriage is at right. Set carriage for 1×1 rib knitting. Set RC at 000. Using MT-7/MT-7, K 23 rows. Transfer sts for st st. Using WY, K a few rows and release from machine.
Machines without ribber
Push 152 Ns to WP. With K side facing, pick up sts around neck edge and place on to Ns. Set RC at 000. Using MT and C, K 1 row.

Transfer every 3rd st on to adjacent N and push empty Ns to NWP. Using MT-3, K 4 rows. Using MT-4, K 11 rows. Using MT-3, K 3 rows. Push Ns from NWP to WP and place loop from row below adjacent st on to empty Ns. Using MT, K 2 rows. Using WY, K a few rows and release from machine.

TO JOIN SLEEVES AND ARMHOLES
Push 156 Ns to WP. With K side facing, replace 156 sts from top of sleeve on to Ns. Wiith P side facing, pick up 156 sts along side of armhole and place on to same Ns. Using MT and MC, K 1 row. Cast off (bind off).

PRESSING
With wrong side facing, pin out pieces to measurements given. Press carefully following instructions on cone band.

MAKING UP
Sew rows above markers on sleeves to cast off (bound off) sts on back and fronts. Join side and sleeve seams. Graft lower edge of pockets into position. Sew side edges of pockets into position.
Machines with ribber
Pin neckband into position. Unravelling WY as required, backstitch through open loops of last row worked in C. Fold in half to inside and slipstitch down.
Machines without ribber
Fold in half to right side and pin into position. Unravelling WY as required, backstitch through open loops of last row worked in C.
All machines
Neaten open ends of bands. Finish buttonholes and sew on buttons.

Babe Ruth Skirt

This skirt is a feminine alternative to
the baseball image, and is simple to make.

PATTERN RATING
● Easy to knit.

MACHINES
This pattern is suitable for standard gauge
machines.

MATERIALS
Brockwell's Lambswool 3 ply (scoured).
260 [290, 320] g (9½ [10½, 11½] oz) in Black
(MC).
Elastic to fit waist.
*Brockwell's Lambswool 3 ply is 100% Pure
Lambswool.*

YARN THICKNESS
Medium fine yarn.

MEASUREMENTS
To fit hips 87-92 [97-102, 102-107] cm, 34-36
[38-40, 40-42] in.
Actual measurement 94 [104, 114] cm, 37 [41,
45] in.
Length 52.5 cm, 20¾ in.
*Instructions are written for the smallest size,
larger sizes follow in square brackets. If only
one figure is given, it applies to all sizes.*

TENSION
26 stitches and 41 rows to 10 cm, 4 in
measured over stocking stitch (tension dial
setting approximately 7).
*For perfect results, your tension must be
matched exactly before starting the
garment.*

ABBREVIATIONS
See page 9.

NOTES
Knit side of knitting is right side of finished
garment.

BACK AND FRONT (Alike)
Machines with ribber
With ribber in position and carriage at right,
set machine for 1×1 rib. Using MC, cast on
124 [138, 150] sts in 1×1 rib. K 3 tubular
rows. Carriage is at right. Set carriage for
1×1 rib knitting. Set RC at 000. Using
MT-7/MT-7, K 12 rows. Transfer sts for st st.
Machines without ribber
Push 125 [140, 152] Ns to WP. Push every 3rd
N back to NWP. Using MT and WY, cast on
and K a few rows ending with carriage at

*Baseball cardigan and Babe Ruth suit –
complementary his and her outfits.*

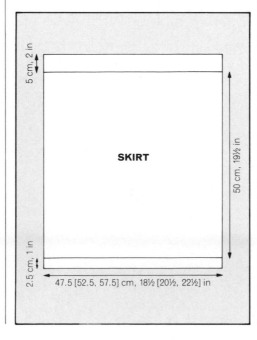

5 cm, 2 in

50 cm, 19½ in

SKIRT

2.5 cm, 1 in

47.5 [52.5, 57.5] cm, 18½ [20½, 22½] in

left. Set RC at 000. Using MT-4 and MC, K
23 rows. Push Ns from NWP to WP and
make a hem by placing loops of first row
worked in MC evenly along the row. Unravel
WY when work is completed.
1st size Dec 1 st at right edge.
2nd and 3rd sizes Dec 1 st at each end.
All sizes 124 [138, 150] sts.
All machines
Set RC at 000. Using MT, K 206 rows. Work
measures 52.5 cm, 20¾ in.
Machines without ribber
1st size Inc 1 st at right edge.
2nd and 3rd sizes Inc 1 st at each end.
All sizes 125 [140, 152] sts.
All machines Using WY, K a few rows and
release from machine.

WAISTBAND (Two pieces)
Machines with ribber
With ribber in position and carriage at right,
set machine for 1×1 rib. Using MC, cast on
124 [138, 150] sts in 1×1 rib. K 3 tubular
rows. Carriage is at right. Set carriage for
1×1 rib knitting. Set RC at 000. Using
MT-7/MT-7, K 51 rows. Transfer sts for st st.
Machines without ribber
Push 125 [140, 152] Ns to WP. Push every 3rd
N back to NWP. Using MT and WY, cast on
and K a few rows ending with carriage at
left. Set RC at 000. Using MT-4 and MC, K
47 rows. Push Ns from NWP to WP and
make a hem by placing loops of first row
worked in MC evenly along the row. Unravel
WY when work is completed.
All machines
With P side facing, replace sts from top of
back or front on to Ns. Using MT and MC, K
1 row. Cast off (bind off).

PRESSING
With wrong side facing, pin out pieces to
measurements given. Press carefully
following instructions on cone band.

MAKING UP
Machines with ribber
Join side seams. Fold waistband in half to
inside and slipstitch down, leaving a small
opening. Insert elastic and join ends. Close
opening.
Machines without ribber
Join side seams, leaving a small opening for
elastic. Insert elastic and join ends then
close opening.

35

Baseball

A practical cardigan with obvious references
to the classic baseball jacket. The inset collar stripe
also appears on the ribs.

36 PATTERN RATING
● Easy to knit.

MACHINES
This pattern is suitable for standard gauge
machines.

MATERIALS
Brockwell's Lambswool 3 ply (scoured).
275 [300, 325] g (10[11, 12] oz) in Cardinal
(MC).
210 [230, 250] g (9[8½, 9] oz) in Light Grey
(C).
7 buttons.
*Brockwell's Lambswool 3 ply is 100% Pure
Lambswool.*

YARN THICKNESS
Medium fine yarn.

MEASUREMENTS
To fit chest 92-97 [102-107, 112-117] cm, 36-38
[40-42, 44-46] in.
Actual measurements 106 [116, 126] cm, 41¾
[45¾, 49½] in.
Length to shoulder 68 cm, 26¾ in.
Sleeve seam 49.5 cm, 19½ in.
*Instructions are written for the smallest size,
larger sizes follow in square brackets. If only
one figure is given, it applies to all sizes.*

TENSION
26 stitches and 41 rows to 10 cm, 4 in
measured over stocking stitch (tension dial
setting approximately 7).
*For perfect results, tension must be
matched exactly before starting the
garment.*

ABBREVIATIONS
See page 9.

NOTES
Knit side of knitting is right side of finished
garment.

BACK
Machines with ribber
With ribber in position and carriage at right,
set machine for 1×1 rib. Using MC, cast on
122 [136, 148] sts in 1×1 rib.
* K 3 tubular rows. Carriage is at right. Set
carriage for 1×1 rib knitting. Set RC at 000.
Using MT-7/MT-7, K 4 rows. Using C, K 6
rows. Using MC, K 14 rows. Transfer sts for
st st *.

Machines without ribber

Push 122 [134, 146] Ns to WP.
* Push every 3rd N back to NWP. Using MT and WY, cast on and K a few rows ending with carriage at left. Set RC at 000. Using MT-4 and MC, K 26 rows. Using C, K 5 rows. Using MC, K 12 rows. Push Ns from NWP to WP and make a hem by placing loops of first row worked in MC evenly along the row. Unravel WY when work is completed *.

2nd and 3rd sizes Inc 1 st at each end.
All sizes 122 [136, 148] sts.

All machines
Set RC at 000. Using MT, K 14 rows. Shape sides by inc 1 st at each end of next and every foll 15th row until there are 140 [154, 166] sts. K 11 rows. RC shows 146 and work measures 40 cm, 15¾ in.

Shape armholes Cast off (bind off) 23 sts at beg of next 2 rows. 94 [108, 120] sts. K 108 rows.

Shape neck Using a length of MC, cast off (bind off) centre 52 sts. Push 21 [28, 34] Ns at left to HP and cont on rem sts for first side.
K 1 row. Dec 1 st at beg of next and foll alt row. 19 [26, 32] sts. K 2 rows. Using WY, K a few rows and release from machine.
With carriage at left, push rem Ns from HP to UWP and finish to correspond with first side reversing shapings.

RIGHT FRONT
Machines with ribber
With ribber in position and carriage at right, set machine for 1×1 rib. Using MC, cast on 58 [65, 71] sts in 1×1 rib. Work as for back from * to *.

Machines without ribber
Push 56 [65, 71] Ns to WP. Work as for back from * to *.

1st size Inc 1 st at each end.
All sizes 58 [65, 71] sts.

All machines
Set RC at 000. Using MT, K 14 rows. Shape side by inc 1 st at right edge (left edge on left front) of next and every foll 15th row until there are 67 [74, 80] sts. K 11 rows. RC shows 146 and work measures 40 cm, 15¾ in. K 1 row extra for left front only.

Shape armhole Cast off (bind off) 23 sts at beg of next row. 44 [51, 57] sts. K 78 rows.

Shape neck Cast off (bind off) 7 sts at beg of next row. Dec 1 st (2 sts in) at neck edge of next and every foll alt row until 19 [26, 32] sts rem. K 1 row. Using WY, K a few rows and release from machine.

LEFT FRONT
Work as for right front reversing shapings by noting alteration in number of rows worked.

SLEEVES
Machines with ribber
With ribber in position and carriage at right, set machine for 1×1 rib. Using MC, cast on 62 sts in 1×1 rib. Work as for back from * to *.

Machines without ribber
Push 62 Ns to WP. Work as for back from * to *.

All machines
Set RC at 000. Using MT and C, K 3 rows. Shape sides by inc 1 st (2 sts in) at each end of next and every foll 4th row until there are 146 sts. K 18 rows. RC shows 186 and work measures 49.5 cm, 19½ in. Place marker at each end. K 36 rows. Using WY, K a few rows and release from machine.

POCKETS
Push 38 Ns to WP. Using MT and WY, cast on and K a few rows ending with carriage at left. Set RC at 000. Using MC, K 58 rows. Using WY, K a few rows and release from machine.

POCKET TOPS
Machines with ribber
With ribber in position and carriage at right, set machine for 1×1 rib. Using MC, cast on 38 sts in 1×1 rib. K 3 tubular rows. Carriage is at right. Set carriage for 1×1 rib knitting. Set RC at 000. Using MT-7/MT-7, K 10 rows. Transfer sts for st st.

Machines without ribber
Push 38 Ns to WP. Push every 3rd N back to NWP. Using MT and WY, cast on and K a few rows ending with carriage at left. Set RC at 000. Using MT-4 and MC, K 19 rows. Push Ns from NWP to WP and make a hem by placing loops of first row worked in MC evenly along the row. Unravel WY when work is completed.

All machines
With P side facing, replace sts from top of pocket on to Ns. Using MT and MC, K 1 row. Cast off (bind off).

TO JOIN RIGHT SHOULDER
Push 19 [26, 32] Ns to WP. With K side of right back shoulder facing, replace sts on to Ns. With P side of right front shoulder facing, replace sts on to same Ns. Using MT and MC, K 1 row. Cast off (bind off).

TO JOIN LEFT SHOULDER
Work as for right shoulder but read left for right.

NECKBAND
Machines with ribber
With ribber in position and carriage at right, set machine for 1×1 rib. Using MC, cast on 150 sts in 1×1 rib. K 3 tubular rows. Carriage is at right. Set carriage for 1×1 rib knitting. Set RC at 000. Using MT-7/MT-7, K 39 rows. Using C, K 6 rows. Using MC, K 6 rows. Transfer sts for st st. Using WY, K a few rows and release from machine.

Machines without ribber
Push 152 Ns to WP. With K side facing, pick up 152 sts around neck edge omitting cast off (bound off) sts on front neck and place on to Ns. Set RC at 000. Using MT and MC, K 1 row. Transfer every 3rd st on to adjacent N and push empty Ns to NWP. Using MT-4, K 35 rows. Using C, K 5 rows. Using MC, K 4 rows. Push Ns from NWP to WP and place loop from row below adjacent st on to empty Ns. Using MT, K 2 rows. Using WY, K a few rows and release from machine.

BUTTONHOLE BAND
Machines with ribber
With ribber in position and carriage at right, set machine for 1×1 rib. Using MC, cast on 179 sts in 1×1 rib. K 3 tubular rows. Carriage is at right. Set carriage for 1×1 rib knitting. Set RC at 000. Using MT-6/MT-6, K 7 rows. Counting from left edge, make buttonholes over Ns 5, 6; 15, 16; 47, 48; 79, 80; 111, 112; 143, 144; 175 and 176, K 15 rows. Make buttonholes over same Ns as before. K 7 rows. Transfer sts for st st. Using WY, K a few rows and release from machine.

37

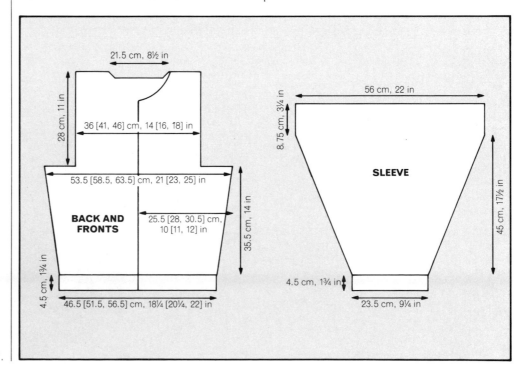

Machines without ribber
Push 154 Ns to WP. With K side facing, pick up sts along left front edge and place on to Ns. Set RC at 000. Using MT-1 and MC, K 6 rows. Counting from left edge, make buttonholes over Ns 4, 5; 11, 12; 39, 40; 67, 68; 95, 96; 123, 124; 151 and 152. K 11 rows. Make buttonholes over same Ns as before. K 6 rows. Transfer sts for st st. Using WY, K a few rows and release from machine.

BUTTON BAND
Machines with ribber
Work as for buttonhole band omitting buttonholes.
Machines without ribber
Work as for buttonhole band omitting buttonholes and read right for left.

TO JOIN SLEEVES TO ARMHOLES
Push 146 Ns to WP. With K side facing, replace 146 sts from top of sleeve on to Ns. With P side facing, pick up 146 sts along side of armhole and place on to same Ns. Using MT and MC, K 1 row. Cast off (bind off).

PRESSING
With wrong side facing, pin out pieces to measurements given. Press carefully following instructions on cone band.

MAKING UP
Sew rows above markers on sleeves to cast off (bound off) sts on back and fronts. Join side and sleeve seams. Graft lower edge of pockets into position. Sew side edges of pockets into position.
Machines with ribber
Pin neckband and front bands into position. Unravelling WY as required, backstitch through open loops of last row worked in MC. Join ends of neckband to cast off (bound off) sts at neck and front bands. Fold bands in half to inside and slipstitch down.
Machines without ribber
Join ends of neckbands to cast off (bound

An ideal beginner's cardigan, Baseball is shown here with Eldorado and Trucking, children's motif sweaters.

off) sts at neck and front bands. Fold in half to right side and pin into position. Unravelling WY as required, backstitch through open loops of last row worked in MC.
All machines
Neaten open ends of bands. Finish buttonholes and sew on buttons.

Eldorado

All the romance of the classic Caddy. You could
easily use this chart in conjunction with a basic adult's pattern.

PATTERN RATING
● ● ● Recommended for experts only.

MACHINES
This pattern is suitable for standard gauge
machines.

MATERIALS
Rowan Botany Wool.
190 g (7 oz) in shade 97 (MC).
80 g (3 oz) in shade 60 (A).
10 g (½ oz) in shade 629 (B).
10 g (½ oz) in shade 12 (C).
10 g (½ oz) in shade 1 (D).
10 g (½ oz) in shade 61 (E).
5 g (¼ oz) in shade 6 (F).
5 g (¼ oz) in shade 62 (G).
*Rowan Botany Wool is 100% Pure New
Wool.*

YARN THICKNESS
Medium yarn.

MEASUREMENTS
To fit chest 66-71 cm, 26-28 in.
Actual measurement 77 cm, 30¼ in.
Length to shoulder 45.5 cm, 18 in.
Sleeve seam 36 cm, 14¼ in.

TENSION
31 stitches and 48 rows to 10 cm, 4 in
measured over stocking stitch (tension dial
setting approximately 5).
*For perfect results, your tension must be
matched exactly before starting the
garment.*

ABBREVIATIONS
See page 9.

NOTES
Knit side of knitting is right side of finished
garment.

BACK
Machines with ribber
With ribber in position and carriage at right,
set machine for 1×1 rib. Push 61 Ns at left
and right of centre 0 to WP. 122 Ns. Push
corresponding Ns on ribber to WP. Arrange
Ns for 1×1 rib. Using A, cast on and K 3
tubular rows. Carriage is at right. Set
carriage for 1×1 rib knitting. Set RC at 000.
Using MT-4/MT-4, K 28 rows. Transfer sts
for st st.
Machines without ribber
Push 61 Ns at left and right of centre 0 to
WP. 122 Ns. Push every 3rd N back to NWP.
Using MT and WY, cast on and K a few rows

ending with carriage at left. Set RC at 000. Using MT-2 and A, K 49 rows. Push Ns from NWP to WP and make a hem by placing loops of first row worked in A evenly along the row. Unravel WY when work is completed.

All machines
Set RC at 000 *.
Using MT, K 76 rows. Using MC, K 26 rows. RC shows 102 and work measures 26 cm, 10¼ in.

Shape armholes Cast off (bind off) 13 sts at beg of next 2 rows. 96 sts. K 86 rows.

Shape neck Using a length of MC, cast off (bind off) centre 56 sts. Push 20 Ns at left to HP and cont on rem sts for first side.
K 1 row. Dec 1 st at beg of next and foll alt row. 18 sts. K 2 rows. Using WY, K a few rows and release from machine.
With carriage at left, push rem Ns from HP to UWP and finish to correspond with first side reversing shapings.

FRONT
Work as for back to *.
Using MT, K 34 rows. Cont in intarsia patt from chart. K 64 rows. Cont in st st and MC, K 4 rows. RC shows 102 and work measures 26 cm, 10¼ in.

Shape armholes Cast off (bind off) 13 sts at beg of next 2 rows. 96 sts. K 72 rows.

Shape neck Using a length of MC, cast off (bind off) centre 44 sts. Push 26 Ns at left to HP and cont on rem sts for first side.
K 1 row. Dec 1 st (2 sts in) at beg of next and

every foll alt row until 18 sts rem. K 4 rows. Using WY, K a few rows and release from machine.
With carriage at left, push rem Ns from HP to UWP and finish to correspond with first side reversing shapings.

SLEEVES
Machines with ribber
With ribber in position and carriage at right, set machine for 1×1 rib. Using MC, cast on 60 sts in 1×1 rib. K 3 tubular rows. Carriage is at right. Set carriage for 1×1 rib knitting. Set RC at 000. Using MT-4/MT-4, K 28 rows. Transfer sts for st st.

Machines without ribber
Push 59 Ns to WP. Push every 3rd N back to NWP. Using MT and WY, cast on and K a

few rows ending with carriage at left. Set RC at 000. Using MT-2 and MC, K 49 rows. Push Ns from NWP to WP and make a hem by placing loops of first row worked in MC evenly along the row. Unravel WY when work is completed. Inc 1 st. 60 sts.

All machines
Set RC at 000. Using MT, K 3 rows. Shape sides by inc 1 st at each end of next and every foll 4th row until there are 122 sts. K 26 rows. RC shows 150 and work measures 36 cm, 14¼ in. Place marker at each end. K 20 rows. Using WY, K a few rows and release from machine.

TO JOIN RIGHT SHOULDER
Push 18 Ns to WP. With K side of right back shoulder facing, replace sts on to Ns. With

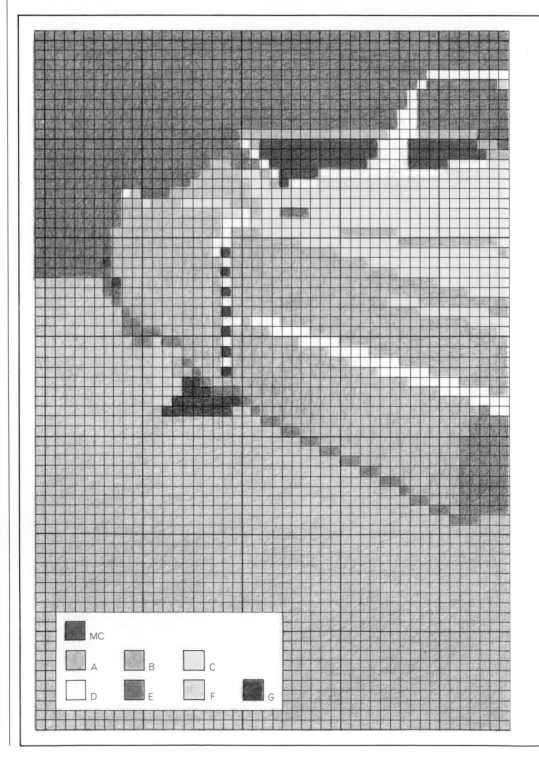

P side of right front shoulder facing, replace sts on to same Ns. Using MT and MC, K 1 row. Cast off (bind off).

NECKBAND
Machines with ribber
With ribber in position and carriage at right, set machine for 1×1 rib. Using MC, cast on 135 sts in 1×1 rib. K 3 tubular rows. Carriage is at right. Set carriage for 1×1 rib knitting. Set RC at 000. Using MT-4/MT-4, K 22 rows. Transfer sts for st st. Using WY, K a few rows and release from machine.

Machines without ribber
Push 137 Ns to WP. With K side facing, pick up 137 sts around neck edge and place on to Ns. Set RC at 000. Using MT and MC, K 1 row. Transfer every 3rd st on to adjacent N

and push empty Ns to NWP. Using MT-1, K 4 rows. Using MT-2, K 9 rows. Using MT-1, K 3 rows. Push Ns from NWP to WP and place a loop from row below adjacent st on to empty Ns. Using MT, K 2 rows. Using WY, K a few rows and release from machine.

TO JOIN LEFT SHOULDER
Work as for right shoulder but read left for right.

TO JOIN SLEEVES TO ARMHOLES
Push 122 Ns to WP. With K side facing, replace 122 sts from top of sleeve on to Ns. With P side facing, pick up 122 sts along side of armhole anmd place on to same Ns. Using MT and MC, K 1 row. Cast off (bind off).

PRESSING
With wrong side facing, pin out pieces to measurements given. Press carefully following instructions on cone band.

MAKING UP
Sew rows above markers on sleeves to cast off (bound off) sts on back and front. Join side, sleeve and neckband seams.

Machines with ribber
Pin neckband into position. Unravelling WY as required, backstitch through open loops of last row worked in MC. Fold in half to inside and stipstich down.

Machines without ribber
Fold neckband in half to right side and pin. Unravelling WY as required, backstitch through open loops of last row worked in MC.

41

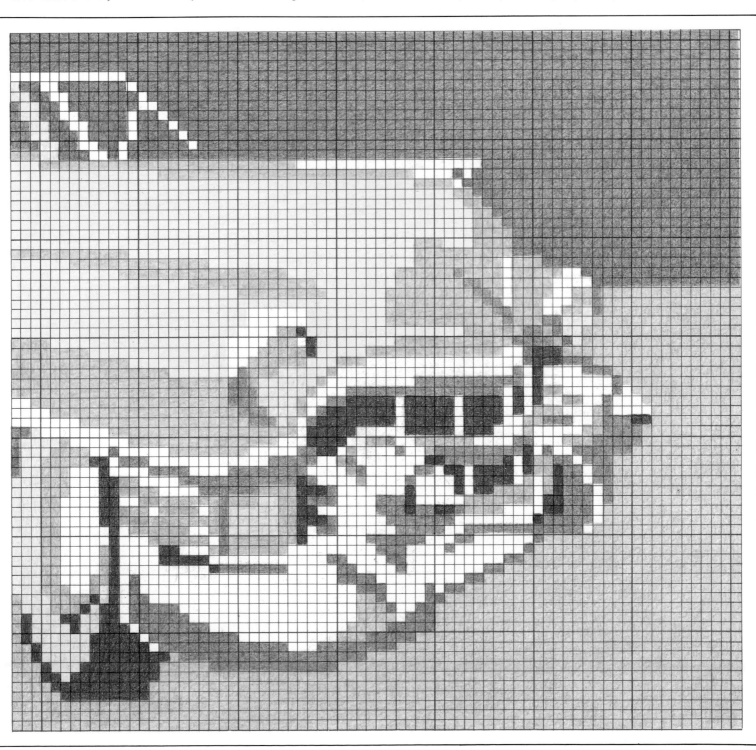

Trucking

This design takes a lot of patience to produce, but the finished effect is always treasured.

42 PATTERN RATING
●●● Recommended for experts only.

MACHINES
This pattern is suitable for standard gauge machines.

MATERIALS
Rowan Botany Wool.
220 g (8 oz) in shade 48 (MC).
95 g (3½ oz) in shade 60 (A).
20 g (1 oz) in shade 64 (B).
20 g (1 oz) in shade 62 (C).
15 g (½ oz) in shade 1 (D).
10 g (½ oz) in shade 44 (E).
10 g (½ oz) in shade 115 (F).
10 g (½ oz) in shade 12 (G).
2 g (¼ oz) in shade 14 (H).
Rowan Botany Wool is 100% Pure New Wool.

YARN THICKNESS
Medium yarn.

MEASUREMENTS
To fit chest 71-76 cm, 28-30 in.
Actual measurement 85 cm, 33½ in.
Length to shoulder 50 cm, 19¾ in.
Sleeve seam 38 cm, 15 in.

TENSION
31 stitches and 48 rows to 10 cm, 4 in measured over stocking stitch (tension dial setting approximately 5).

For perfect results, your tension must be matched exactly before starting the garment.

ABBREVIATIONS
See page 9.

NOTES
Knit side of knitting is right side of finished garment.

BACK
Machines with ribber
With ribber in position and carriage at right, set machine for 1×1 rib. Push 67 Ns at left and right of centre 0 to WP. 134 Ns. Push corresponding Ns on ribber to WP. Arrange Ns for 1×1 rib. Using A, cast on and K 3 tubular rows. Carriage is at right. Set carriage for 1×1 rib knitting. Set RC at 000. Using MT-4/MT-4, K 28 rows. Transfer sts for st st.
Machines without ribber
Push 67 Ns at left and right of centre 0 to WP. 134 Ns. Push every 3rd N back to NWP. Using MT and WY, cast on and K a few rows ending with carriage at left. Set RC at 000. Using MT-2 and A, K 49 rows. Push Ns from NWP to WP and make a hem by placing loops of first row worked in A evenly along the row. Unravel WY when work is completed.
All machines
Set RC at 000 *.

Using MT, K 88 rows. Using MC, K 34 rows. RC shows 122 and work measures 30.5 cm, 12 in.
Shape armholes Cast off (bind off) 16 sts at beg of next 2 rows. 102 sts. K 86 rows.
Shape neck Using a length of MC, cast off (bind off) centre 56 sts. Push 23 Ns at left to HP and cont on rem sts for first side.
K 1 row. Dec 1 st at beg of next and foll alt row, 21 sts. K 2 rows. Using WY, K a few rows and release from machine.
With carriage at left, push rem Ns from HP to UWP and finish to correspond with first side reversing shapings.

FRONT
Work as for back to *.
Using MT, K 36 rows. Cont in intarsia patt from chart. K 86 rows. RC shows 122 and work measures 30.5 cm, 12 in.
Shape armholes Cast off (bind off) 16 sts at beg of next 2 rows. 102 sts. K 11 rows. Cont in st st and MC. K 61 rows.
Shape neck Using a length of MC, cast off (bind off) centre 44 sts. Push 29 Ns at left to HP and cont on rem sts for first side.
K 1 row. Dec 1 st (2 sts in) at beg of next and every foll alt row until 21 sts rem. K 4 rows. Using WY, K a few rows and release from machine.
With carriage at left, push rem Ns from HP to UWP and finish to correspond with first side reversing shapings.

SLEEVES
Machines with ribber
With ribber in position and carriage at right, set machine for 1×1 rib. Using MC, cast on 60 sts in 1×1 rib. K 3 tubular rows. Carriage is at right. Set carriage for 1×1 rib knitting. Set RC at 000. Using MT-4/MT-4, K 28 rows. Transfer sts for st st.
Machines without ribber
Push 59 Ns to WP. Push every 3rd N back to NWP. Using MT and WY, cast on and K a few rows ending with carriage at left. Set RC at 000. Using MT-2 and MC, K 49 rows. Push Ns from NWP to WP and make a hem by placing loops of first row worked in MC

Perfect partners, both Eldorado and Trucking sweaters would be equally acceptable for girls or boys to wear. Choose their favourite colours for the body of the car or truck motifs.

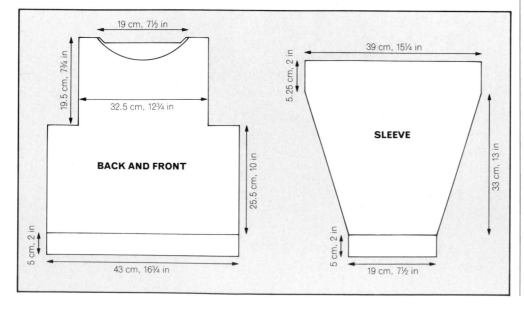

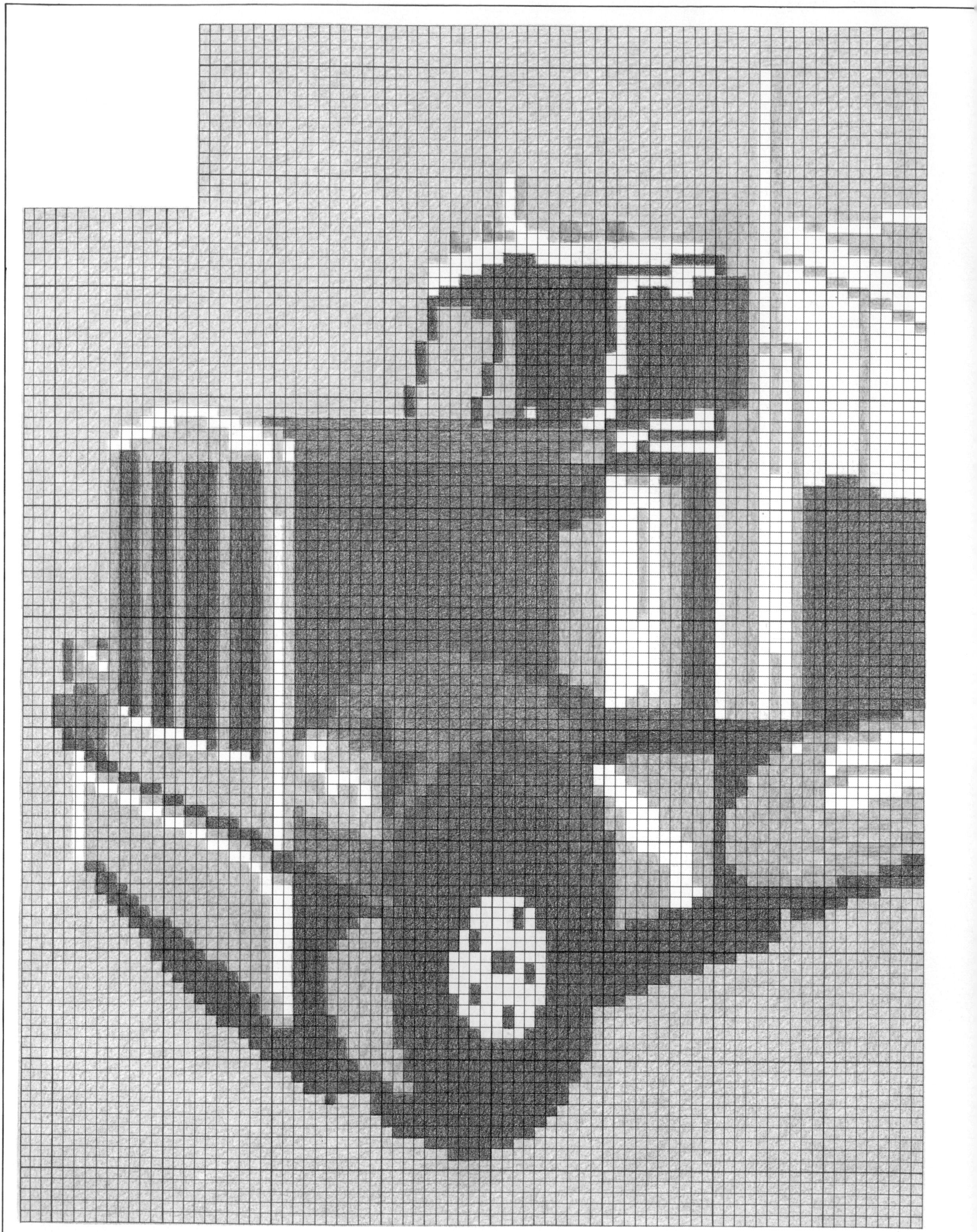

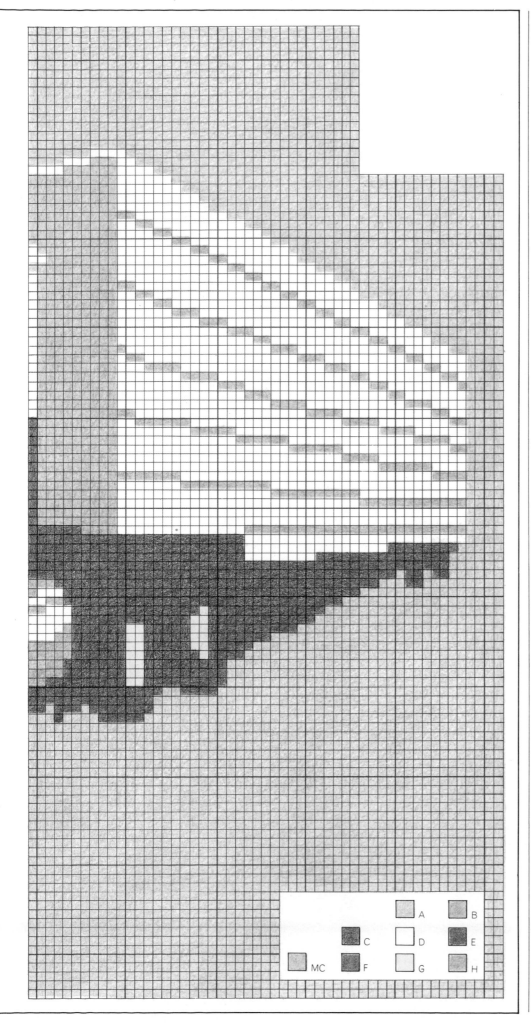

		A	B
	C	D	E
MC	F	G	H

evenly along the row. Unravel WY when work is completed. Inc 1 st. 60 sts.

All machines Set RC at 000. Using MT, K 4 rows. Shape sides by inc 1 st at each end of next and every foll 5th row until there are 122 sts. K 4 rows. RC shows 159 and work measures 38 cm, 15 in. Place marker at each end. K 25 rows. Using WY, K a few rows and release from machine.

TO JOIN RIGHT SHOULDER
Push 21 Ns to WP. With K side of right back shoulder facing, replace sts on to Ns. With P side of right front shoulder facing, replace sts on to same Ns. Using MT and MC, K 1 row. Cast off (bind off).

NECKBAND
Machines with ribber
With ribber in position and carriage at right, set machine for 1×1 rib. Using MC, cast on 135 sts in 1×1 rib. K 3 tubular rows. Carriage is at right. Set carriage for 1×1 rib knitting. Set RC at 000. Using MT-4/MT-4, K 22 rows. Transfer sts for st st. Using WY, K a few rows and release from machine.
Machines without ribber
Push 137 Ns to WP. With K side facing, pick up 137 sts around neck edge and place on to Ns. Set RC at 000. Using MT and MC, K 1 row. Transfer every 3rd st on to adjacent N and push empty Ns to NWP. Using MT-1, K 4 rows. Using MT-2, K 9 rows. Using MT-1, K 3 rows. Push Ns from NWP to WP and place loop from row below adjacent st on to empty Ns. Using MT, K 2 rows. Using WY, K a few rows and release from machine.

TO JOIN LEFT SHOULDER
Work as for right shoulder but read left for right.

TO JOIN SLEEVES TO ARMHOLES
Push 122 Ns to WP. With K side facing, replace 122 sts from top of sleeve on to Ns. Unravel WY. With P side facing, pick up 122 sts along side of armhole and place on to same Ns. Using MT and MC, K 1 row. Cast off (bind off).

PRESSING
With wrong side facing, pin out pieces to measurements given. Press carefully following instructions on cone band.

MAKING UP
Sew rows above markers on sleeves to cast off (bound off) sts on back and front. Join side, sleeve and neckband seams.
Machines with ribber
Pin neckband into position. Unravelling WY as required, backstitch through open loops of last row worked in MC. Fold in half to inside and slipstitch down.
Machines without ribber
Fold neckband in half to right side and pin into position. Unravelling WY as required, backstitch through open loops of last row worked in MC.

New Jersey

Dynamic sports sweater in cotton or wool. It can be made with either a collar or crew neck.

PATTERN RATING
* Easy to knit.

MACHINES
This pattern is suitable for standard gauge machines.

MATERIALS
Rowan Soft Cotton.
SWEATER WITH COLLAR
295 g (10½ oz) in shade 526 (MC).
275 g (10 oz) in shade 535 (C).
CREW NECK SWEATER
295 g (10½ oz) in shade 540 (MC).
275 g (10 oz) in shade 522 (C).
Rowan Soft Cotton is 100% Pure Cotton.

YARN THICKNESS
Medium yarn.

MEASUREMENTS
To fit chest 97-107 cm, 38-42 in.
Actual measurement 114 cm, 45 in.
Length to shoulder 70 cm, 27½ in.
Sleeve seam 49.5 cm, 19½ in.

TENSION
31.5 stitches and 44 rows to 10 cm, 4 in measured over stocking stitch (tension dial setting approximately 5).
For perfect results, your tension must be matched exactly before starting the garment.

ABBREVIATIONS
See page 9.

NOTES
Knit side of knitting is right side of finished garment.

BACK
Machines with ribber
With ribber in position and carriage at right, set machine for 1×1 rib. Using MC, cast on 182 sts in 1×1 rib.
* K 3 tubular rows. Carriage is at right. Set carriage for 1×1 rib knitting. Set RC at 000. Using MT-5/MT-5, K 22 rows. Transfer sts for st st *.
Machines without ribber
Push 182 Ns to WP.

The green and white sweater has a plain crew neck, whilst the yellow and black striped sweater has a neat ribbed collar.

* Push every 3rd N back to NWP. Using MT and WY, cast on and K a few rows ending with carriage at left. Set RC at 000. Using MT-2 and MC, K 43 rows. Push Ns from NWP to WP and make a hem by placing loops of first row worked in MC evenly along the row. Unravel WY when work is completed *.
All machines
Set RC at 000. Using MT, cont in stripes of 20 rows C and 20 rows MC, K 160 rows. Work measures 40.5 cm, 16 in.
Shape armholes Cast off (bind off) 16 sts at beg of next 2 rows. 150 sts **.
K 122 rows.
Shape neck Using a length of C, cast off (bind off) centre 66 sts. Push 42 Ns at left to HP and cont on rem sts for first side.
K 1 row. Dec 1 st at beg of next and foll alt row. 40 sts. K 2 rows. Using WY, K a few rows and release from machine.
With carriage at left, push rem Ns from HP to UWP. Finish to correspond with first side reversing shapings.

FRONT
Work as for back to **.
K 99 rows.
Shape neck Using a length of MC, cast off (bind off) centre re 46 sts. Push 52 Ns at right to HP and cont on rem sts for first side.
K 1 row. Dec 1 st at beg of next and every foll

alt row until 40 sts rem. K 5 rows. Using WY, K a few rows and release from machine.
With carriage at right, push rem Ns from HP to UWP. Finish to correspond with first side reversing shapings.

SLEEVES
Machines with ribber
With ribber in position and carriage at right, set machine for 1×1 rib . Using MC, cast on 74 sts in 1×1 rib. Work as for back from * to *.
Machines without ribber
Push 74 Ns to WP. Work as for back from * to *.
All machines
Set RC at 000. Using MT, cont in stripes of 20 rows C and 20 rows MC, K 2 rows. Shape sides by inc 1 st at each end of next and every foll 3rd row until there are 186 sts. K 30 rows. RC shows 198 and work measures 49.5 cm, 19½ in. Place marker at each end. K 22 rows. Using WY, K a few rows and release from machine.

JOIN RIGHT SHOULDER
Push 40 Ns to WP. With K side of right back shoulder facing, replace sts on to Ns. With P side of right front shoulder facing, replace sts on to same Ns. Unravel WY. Using MT and C, K 1 row. Cast off (bind off).

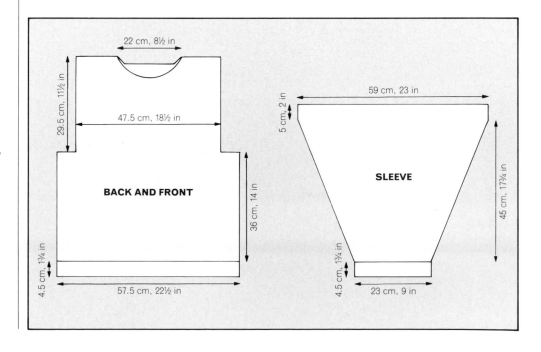

evenly along the row.
Unravel WY when work is completed. Using MT, K 2 rows. Using WY, K a few rows and release from machine.

NECKBAND
Machines with ribber
With ribber in position and carriage at right, set machine for 1×1 rib. Using C, cast on 156 sts in 1×1 rib. K 3 tubular rows. Carriage is at right. Set carriage for 1×1 rib knitting. Set RC at 000. Using MT-5/MT-5, K 28 rows. Transfer sts for st st. Using WY, K a few rows and release from machine.

Machines without ribber
Push 158 Ns to WP. With K side facing, pick up 158 sts around neck edge and place on to Ns. Using MT and C, K 1 row. Transfer every 3rd st on to adjacent N and push empty Ns to NWP. Using MT-1, K 5 rows. Using MT-2, K 13 rows. Using MT-1, K 4 rows. Push Ns from NWP to WP and place loop from row below adjacent st on to empty Ns. Using MT, K 2 rows. Using WY, K a few rows and release from machine.

TO JOIN LEFT SHOULDER
Work as for right shoulder reading left for right.

TO JOIN SLEEVES TO ARMHOLES
Push 186 Ns to WP. With K side of sleeve facing, replace 186 sts on to Ns. With P side of armhole facing, pick up 186 sts along side edge and place on to same Ns. Unravel WY. Using MT and MC, K 1 row. Cast off (bind off).

PRESSING
With wrong side facing, pin out all pieces to measurements given. Press carefully following instructions on cone band.

MAKING UP
Sew rows above markers on sleeves to cast off (bound off) sts on back and front. Join side and sleeve seams.
SWEATER WITH COLLAR
Pin collar into position with ends at centre front. Unravelling WY as required, backstitch through open loops of last row worked in MC.
Machines without ribber
Neaten ends of collar.
CREW NECK SWEATER
Join neckband seam.
Machines with ribber
Pin neckband into position. Unravelling WY as required, backstitch through open loops of last row worked in C. Fold in half to inside and slipstitch down.
Machines without ribber
Fold neckband in half to right side and pin in position. Unravelling WY as required, backstitch through open loops of last row worked in C.
All machines
Join row ends of the collar at centre front for approx 2.5 cm, 1 in.

COLLAR
Machines with ribber
With ribber in position and carriage at right, set machine for 1×1 rib. Using MC, cast on 156 sts in 1×1 rib. K 3 tubular rows. Carriage is at right. Set carriage for 1×1 rib knitting. Set RC at 000. Using MT-5/MT-5, K 54 rows. Transfer sts for st st. Using WY, K a few rows and release from machine.

Machines without ribber
Push 158 Ns to WP. Push every 3rd N back to NWP. Using MT and WY, cast on and K a few rows ending with carriage at left. Set RC at 000. Using MT-2 and MC, K 93 rows. Push Ns from NWP to WP and make a hem by placing loops of first row worked in MC

Down to Earth

This section comprises strong graphic motifs suggesting leaves, carrots and fish. The fourth pattern is a relatively simple Shetland sweater and skirt.

As an alternative to flower motifs I designed the carrot sweater. Initially I drew bunches of carrots with tops, finally reducing the drawings to a stylized carrot, which has a stencilled and almost cartoon character. The pattern is most successful if you keep the outline of the carrot black or, at least, a very dark colour. The background then works with any colour. In this case, I have knitted it in an obvious carrot colour, a burnt-orange flecked yarn, which enhances the earthy feel. The design is also successful with plain yarns.

For the Fish Bone sweater I tried to suggest skeletal patterns, reducing them to very basic outlines. It looks more complicated than the carrot but, because it's a single-colour pattern, it's no more difficult to knit on an electronic machine. Again, the fish outline is best kept black so that any colour works as a background, although the flecked blue yarn gives the pattern added depth. The Fish Bone pattern could be developed into a single motif on a child's sweater by omitting the black dashes around the fish. In this case the fish outline could be any colour.

An exhibition of Eric Ravilious' decorative pottery and woodcuts inspired the treatment of the leaf motif in the Windfall design. The shape of the cardigan is short and boxy, although if you are fairly experienced, you can readily lengthen it. The ribs are narrow so that they cut into the pattern as little as possible.

The Windfall Dress, which can be worn with the cardigan, is by contrast totally plain, to set off the flecked yarn to maximum effect. It is shaped slightly at the waist with a turn-over collar and deep armholes narrowing down to the cuff. The length can be altered by changing the number of rows above the hem rib.

Shetland yarn has a subtle blending of colours and flecks, so it's easy to mix colours which, although different, contain elements of each other. It forms a perfect base for the Shetland design which has two large areas of colour blending into a fringe where they meet. You could reverse the colours of the sweater and have the brighter colour on top. It has a V-neck with overlapping inset collar, which can be turned down or left snug around the neck.

The skirts worn with the jumpers are very easy to make – try combining a neutral and a bright colour, which makes the skirt quite practical if worn with something else.

Shetland

The two flecked yarns create a subtle blending of colours, enhanced by the fringe pattern. The V-neck, with overlapping inset collar, can be turned down or left snug around the neck.

PATTERN RATING
●● Fairly easy, for knitters with some experience.

MACHINES
This pattern is suitable for standard gauge punchcard machines.

MATERIALS
2/8's Shetland (scoured).
475 g (17 oz) in grey (MC).
100 g (3½ oz) in yellow (C).

YARN THICKNESS
Medium yarn.

MEASUREMENTS
To fit 87-97 cm, 34-38 in.
Actual measurement 127 cm, 50 in.
Length to shoulder 76 cm, 30 in.
Sleeve seam 40 cm, 15¾ in.

TENSION
28 stitches and 37 rows to 10 cm, 4 in measured over stocking stitch (tension dial setting approximately 8).
For perfect results, your tension must be matched exactly before starting the garment.

ABBREVIATIONS
See page 9.

NOTES
Knit side of knitting is right side of finished garment.
The card shown on page 54 should be punched, if required, before starting to knit.

BACK
Machines with ribber
With ribber in position and carriage at right, set machine for 1×1 rib. Push 80 Ns at left and right of centre 0 to WP. 160 Ns.
* Push corresponding Ns on ribber to WP. Arrange Ns for 1×1 rib. Using C, cast on and K 3 tubular rows. Carriage is at right. Set carriage for 1×1 rib knitting. Set RC at 000. Using MT-7/MT-7, K 14 rows. Transfer sts for st st *.

Alternative colourways are seen here, showing that the skirt can match either colour in the jersey. The original colours of yellow and grey are shown overleaf.

Machines without ribber
Push 79 Ns at left and right of centre 0 to WP. 158 Ns.
* Push every 3rd N back to NWP. Using MT and WY, cast on and K a few rows ending with carriage at left. Set RC at 000. Using MT-2 and C, K 25 rows. Push Ns from NWP to WP and make a hem by placing loops of first row worked in C evenly along the row. Unravel WY when work is completed. *.
Inc 1 st at each end. 160 sts.

All machines
Insert punchcard and lock on first row. Set RC at 000. Using MT, shape sides by inc 1 st at each end of every 15th row until there are 172 sts. Release card and cont in Fair Isle patt with C in feeder 1(A) and MC in feeder 2(B). Using MT+1, cont to inc on every 15th row from previous inc until there are 176 sts. K 2 rows. Cont in st st. Using MT and MC, cont to inc on every 15th row from previous inc until there are 180 sts. K 6 rows. RC shows 156 and work measures 45 cm, 17¾ in.
Shape armholes Cast off (bind off) 25 sts at beg of next 2 rows. 130 sts **.
K 108 rows.
Shape neck Using a length of MC, cast off (bind off) centre 58 sts. Push Ns at left to HP and cont on rem sts for first side.
K 1 row. Dec 1 st at beg of next and foll alt row. 34 sts. K 2 rows. Using WY, K a few rows and release from machine.
With carriage at left, push Ns from HP to UWP. Finish to correspond with first side reversing shapings.

FRONT
Work as for back to **.
K 52 rows.
Shape neck Push 65 Ns at left to HP and cont on rem sts for first side.
K 1 row. Dec 1 st at beg of next and every foll alt row until 34 sts rem. Using WY, K a few rows and release from machine.
With carriage at left, push Ns from HP to UWP. Finish to correspond with first side reversing shapings.

SLEEVES
Machines with ribber
With ribber in position and carriage at right, set machine for 1×1 rib. Push 30 Ns at left and right of centre 0 to WP. 60 Ns. Work as for back from * to *.
Machines without ribber
Push 30 Ns at left and 29 Ns at right of centre 0 to WP. 59 Ns. Work as for back from * to *. Inc 1 st at right edge. 60 sts.
All machines
Insert punchcard and lock on first row. Set RC at 000. Using MT, shape sides by inc 1 st at each end of every alt row until there are 122 sts. Release card and cont in Fair Isle patt with C in feeder 1(A) and MC in feeder 2(B). Using MT+1, cont to inc on every alt row from previous inc until there are 154 sts. Cont in st st. Using MT and MC, cont to inc

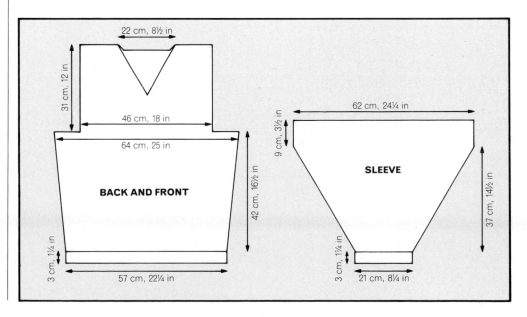

BACK AND FRONT

22 cm, 8½ in
31 cm, 12 in
46 cm, 18 in
64 cm, 25 in
42 cm, 16½ in
3 cm, 1¼ in
57 cm, 22¼ in

SLEEVE

62 cm, 24¼ in
9 cm, 3½ in
37 cm, 14½ in
3 cm, 1¼ in
21 cm, 8¼ in

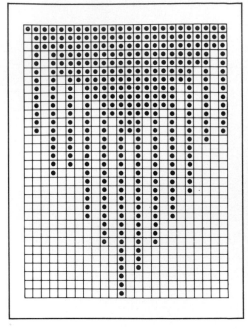

on every alt row from previous inc until there are 174 sts. K 24 rows. RC shows 138 and work measures 40 cm, 15¾ in. Place marker at each end. K 34 rows. Using WY, K a few rows and release from machine.

COLLAR
Using MC, cast on 144 sts by hand. Set RC at 000. Using MT, K 76 rows. Cast off (bind off).

TO JOIN RIGHT SHOULDER
Push 34 Ns to WP. With K side of right back shoulder facing, replace sts on to Ns. Unravel WY. With P side of right front shoulder facing, replace sts on to same Ns. Unravel WY. Using MT and MC, K 1 row. Cast off (bind off).

TO JOIN LEFT SHOULDER
Work as for right shoulder, reading left for right.

TO JOIN SLEEVES AND ARMHOLES
Push 174 Ns to WP. With K side facing, replace 174 sts from top of sleeve on to Ns. Unravel WY. With P side facing, pick up 174 sts along side edge of armhole and place on to same Ns. Using MT and MC, K 1 row. Cast off (bind off).

PRESSING
With wrong side facing, pin out to measurements given. Press carefully following instructions on cone/ball band.

MAKING UP
Sew rows above markers on sleeves to cast off (bound off) sts on back and front. Join side and sleeve seams. Fold collar in half lengthways. Sew in position lapping right over left.

Knitted to match the top colour of the sweater, the calf length version of the skirt is seen here.

Shetland Skirts

Two simple and practical skirts which complement
the Shetland sweater.

PATTERN RATING
● ● Fairly easy, for knitters with some
experience.

MACHINES
This pattern is suitable for standard gauge
punchcard machines.

MATERIALS
2/8's Shetland (scoured).
KNEE LENGTH SKIRT
250 g (9 oz) grey (MC). Elastic to fit waist.
CALF LENGTH SKIRT
385 g (14 oz) in grey (MC). Elastic to fit waist.

YARN THICKNESS
Medium yarn.

MEASUREMENTS
Actual measurement 90 cm, 35½ in.
Knee length 53.5 cm, 21 in.
Calf length 77.5 cm, 30½ in.

TENSION
28 stitches and 37 rows to 10 cm, 4 in
measured over stocking stitch (tension dial
setting approximately 8).
*For perfect results, your tension must be
matched exactly before starting the
garment.*

ABBREVIATIONS
See page 9.

NOTES
Knit side of knitting is right side of finished
garment.

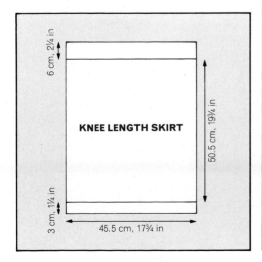

KNEE LENGTH SKIRT

6 cm, 2¼ in · 50.5 cm, 19¾ in · 3 cm, 1¼ in · 45.5 cm, 17¾ in

KNEE LENGTH SKIRT
(Back and front alike)
Machines with ribber
With ribber in position and carriage at right,
set machine for 1×1 rib. Using MC, cast on
128 sts in 1×1 rib. K 3 tubular rows. Carriage
is at right. Set carriage for 1×1 rib knitting.
Set RC at 000. Using MT-7/MT-7, K 14 rows.
Transfer sts for st st. Set RC at 000 *.
Using MT, K 188 rows.
Machines without ribber
Using MC, cast on 128 sts by hand. Using
MT-1, K 12 rows. Set RC at 000 *.
Using MT, K 200 rows.
All machines
Using WY, K a few rows and release from
machine.

WAISTBAND
(Two pieces)
Machines with ribber
With ribber in position and carriage at right,
set machine for 1×1 rib. Using MC, cast on
128 sts in 1×1 rib. K 3 tubular rows. Carriage
is at right. Set carriage for 1×1 rib knitting.
Set RC at 000. Using MT-7/MT-7, K 60 rows.
Transfer sts for st st.
Machines without ribber
Push 128 Ns to WP. Push every 3rd N back
to NWP. Using MT and WY, cast on and K a
few rows ending with carriage at left. Set RC
at 000. Using MT-2 and MC, K 49 rows.
Push Ns from NWP to WP and make a hem
by placing loops of first row worked in MC
evenly along the row. Unravel WY when
work is completed.
All machines
With P side of skirt facing, replace sts on to
Ns. Using MT, K 1 row. Cast off (bind off).

PRESSING
Press as for sweater.

MAKING UP
Machines with ribber
Join side seams. Fold waistband in half and
slipstitch down on inside, leaving an
opening for elastic.
Machines without ribber
Join side seams, leaving an opening for
elastic. Turn up 12 rows at lower edge and
slipstitch down on inside.
All machines
Insert elastic into waistband and join ends.
Close openings.

CALF LENGTH SKIRT
(Back and front alike)
Machines with ribber
Work as for knee length skirt to *.
Using MT, K 277 rows.
Machines without ribber
Work as for knee length skirt to *.
Using MT, K 289 rows.
All machines
Using WY, K a few rows and release from
machine.

WAISTBAND (Two pieces)
Work as for knee length skirt.

PRESSING
Press as for sweater.

MAKING UP
Work as for knee length skirt.

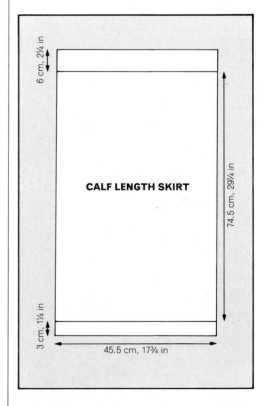

CALF LENGTH SKIRT

6 cm, 2¼ in · 74.5 cm, 29¾ in · 3 cm, 1¼ in · 45.5 cm, 17¾ in

Fish Bone

This repeated fish-bone pattern works with almost any background colour. Knitted in a cotton yarn, it would make a cool spring sweater.

PATTERN RATING
●● Fairly easy, for knitters with some experience.

MACHINES
This pattern is suitable for electronic machines.

MATERIALS
Rowan Fine Fleck Tweed.
400 g (14½ oz) in shade 56 (MC).
125 g (4½ oz) in shade 97 (C).

Rowan Fine Fleck Tweed is 75% Pure New Wool base, 15% Cotton Nepp, 10% Nylon.

YARN THICKNESS
Medium yarn.

MEASUREMENTS
To fit chest 97-107 cm, 38-42 in.
Actual measurement 125 cm, 49¼ in.
Length to shoulder 70 cm, 27½ in.
Sleeve seam 56 cm, 22 in.

TENSION
28.5 stitches and 38.5 rows to 10 cm, 4 in measured over Fair Isle pattern (tension dial setting approximately 7).
For perfect results, your tension must be matched exactly before starting the garment.

ABBREVIATIONS
See page 9.

NOTES
Knit side of knitting is right side of finished garment.
Fill in pattern card shown on page 58 before starting to knit.

BACK
Machines with ribber
With ribber in position and carriage at right, set machine for 1×1 rib. Push 84 Ns at left and right of centre 0 to WP. 168 Ns.
* Push corresponding Ns on ribber to WP. Arrange Ns for 1×1 rib. Using MC, cast on and K 3 tubular rows. Carriage is at right. Insert card and lock on first row. Set carriage for 1×1 rib knitting. Set RC at 000. Using MT-6/MT-6, K 26 rows. Transfer sts for st st *.
Machines without ribber
Push 84 Ns at left and 83 Ns at right of centre 0 to WP. 167 Ns.
* Push every 3rd N back to NWP. Using MT and WY, cast on and K a few rows ending with carriage at left. Insert card and lock on first row. Set RC at 000. Using MT-2 and

MC, K 37 rows. Push Ns from NWP to WP and make a hem by placing loops of first row worked in MC evenly along the row. Unravel WY when work is completed *.
Inc 1 st at right edge. 168 sts.
All machines
Set RC at 000. Using MT, K 1 row. Release card and cont in Fair Isle patt with MC in feeder 1(A) and C in feeder 2 (B), K 18 rows. Shape sides by inc 1 st at each end of next and every foll 20th row until there are 180 sts, K 32 rows. RC shows 152 and work measures 43 cm, 17 in.
Shape armholes Cast off (bind off) 12 sts at beg of next 2 rows. 156 sts **.
K 94 rows.
Shape neck Note patt row on card. Using a length of MC, cast off (bind off) centre 56 sts. Using nylon cord, K 50 sts at left by hand taking Ns down to NWP. Cont on rem sts for first side.
K 1 row. Dec 1 st at beg of next and foll alt row. 48 sts. K 2 rows. Cont in st st and MC, K 2 rows. Using WY, K a few rows and release from machine.
With carriage at right, unravel nylon cord over rem Ns bringing Ns back to WP. Lock card on number previously noted. Take carriage to left without knitting. Release card and cont in Fair Isle patt. Finish to correspond with first side reversing shapings.

FRONT
Work as for back to **.
K 74 rows.
Shape neck Note patt row on card. Using a length of MC, cast off (bind off) centre 34 sts. Using nylon cord, K 61 sts at left by hand taking Ns down to NWP. Cont on rem sts for first side.
K 1 row. Dec 1 st at beg of next and every foll alt row until 48 sts rem. Cont in st st and MC. K 2 rows. Using WY, K a few rows and release from machine.
With carriage at right, unravel nylon cord over rem Ns, bringing Ns back to WP. Lock card on number previously noted. Take carriage to left without knitting. Release

57

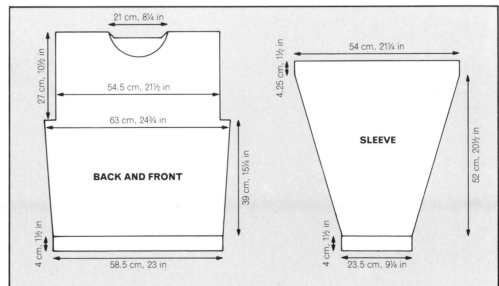

BACK AND FRONT — 21 cm, 8¼ in; 27 cm, 10½ in; 54.5 cm, 21½ in; 63 cm, 24¾ in; 39 cm, 15¼ in; 4 cm, 1½ in; 58.5 cm, 23 in

SLEEVE — 54 cm, 21¼ in; 4.25 cm, 1½ in; 52 cm, 20½ in; 4 cm, 1½ in; 23.5 cm, 9¼ in

card and cont in Fair Isle patt. Finish to correspond with first side reversing shapings.

SLEEVES
Machines with ribber
With ribber in position and carriage at right, set machine for 1×1 rib. Push 34 Ns at left and right of centre 0 to WP. 68 Ns. Work as for back from * to *.
Machines without ribber
Push 34 Ns at left and right of centre 0 to WP. 68 Ns. Work as for back from * to *.
All machines Set RC at 000. Using MT, K 1 row. Release card and cont in Fair Isle patt with MC in feeder 1(A) and C in feeder 2(B), K 2 rows. Shape sides by inc 1 st at each end of next and every foll 4th row until there are 154 sts. K 28 rows. RC shows 200 and work measures 56 cm, 22 in. Place marker at each end. K 15 rows. Cont in st st and MC, K 2 rows. Using WY, K a few rows and release from machine.

TO JOIN RIGHT SHOULDER
Push 48 Ns to WP. With K side of right back shoulder facing, replace sts on to Ns. Unravel WY. With P side of right front shoulder facing, replace sts on to same Ns. Unravel WY. Using MT and MC, K 1 row. Cast off (bind off).

NECKBAND
Machines with ribber
With ribber in position and carriage at right, set machine for 1×1 rib. Using MC, cast on 150 sts in 1×1 rib. K 3 tubular rows. Carriage is at right. Set carriage for 1×1 rib knitting. Set RC at 000. Using MT-6/MT-6, K 24 rows. Transfer sts for st st. With P side facing, pick up 150 sts around neck edge and place on to Ns. Using MT, K 1 row. Cast off (bind off).
Machines without ribber
Push 152 Ns to WP. With K side facing, pick up 152 sts around neck edge and place on to Ns. Set RC at 000. Using MT and MC, K 1 row. Transfer every 3rd st on to adjacent N and push empty Ns to NWP. Using MT-1, K 4 rows. Using MT 2, K 11 rows. Using MT 1, K 3 rows. Push Ns from NWP to WP and place loop from row below adjacent st on to empty Ns. Using MT, K 2 rows. Using WY, K a few rows and release from machine.

TO JOIN LEFT SHOULDER
Work as for right shoulder, reading left for right.

TO JOIN SLEEVES TO ARMHOLES
Push 154 Ns to WP. With K side facing, replace 154 sts from top of sleeve on to Ns. Unravel WY. With P side facing, pick up 154 sts along side edge of armhole and place on to same Ns. Using MT and MC, K 1 row. Cast off (bind off).

PRESSING
With wrong side facing, pin out to measurements given.

Press carefully following the instructions on the cone band.

MAKING UP
Sew the row ends above markers on the sleeves to cast off (bound off) sts on the back and front, then join the side, sleeve and neckband seams.

Machines with ribber
Fold neckband in half to inside and slipstitch down.
Machines without ribber
Fold neckband in half to outside and pin in position. Unravelling WY as required, backstitch through open loops of last row worked in MC.

Carrots

Oversized and warm for winter, the stylized carrot creates a stencilled effect. If desired, change the background colour, keeping the pattern dark.

PATTERN RATING
● ● Fairly easy, for knitters with some experience.

MACHINES
This pattern is written for electronic machines, with or without ribber.

MATERIALS
Rowan Fine Nepp Yarn.
375 [400, 425] g (13½ [14½, 15] oz) in shade 44 (MC).
200 [225, 250] g (7 [8, 9] oz) in shade 62 (C).
Rowan Fine Nepp Yarn is 85% Pure New Wool, 15% Cotton Nepp.

YARN THICKNESS
Medium Yarn.

MEASUREMENTS
To suit chest 87 [92, 97] cm, 34 [38, 42] in.
Actual measurement 115 [125, 135] cm, 45¼, [49¼, 53¼] in.
Length to shoulder 78.5 cm, 31 in.
Sleeve seam 47 cm, 18½ in.
Instructions are written for the smallest size; larger sizes follow in square brackets. If only one figure is given, it applies to all sizes.

TENSION
28.5 stitches and 38.5 rows to 10 cm, 4 in, measured over Fair Isle pattern (tension dial setting approximately 7).
For perfect results, your tension must be matched exactly before starting the garment.

ABBREVIATIONS
See page 9.

NOTES
Knit side of knitting is right side of finished garment.
Fill in pattern card shown on page 62 before starting to knit.

BACK
Machines with ribber
With ribber in position and carriage at right, set machine for 1×1 rib. Push 77 [84, 91] Ns at left and right of centre 0 to WP. 154 [168, 182] Ns.
* Push corresponding Ns on ribber to WP. Arrange Ns for 1×1 rib. Using MC, cast on and K 3 tubular rows. Carriage is at right.

Set carriage for 1×1 rib knitting.
Insert card and lock on first row. Set RC at 000. Using MT-6/MT-6, K 14 rows. Transfer sts for st st *.

Machines without ribber
Insert punchcard and lock on first row. Push 76 [84, 91] Ns at left and 76 [83, 91] Ns at right of centre 0 to WP. 152 [167, 182] Ns.
* Push every 3rd N back to NWP. Using MT and WY, cast on and K a few rows ending with carriage at left. Set RC at 000. Using MT-3 and MC, K 19 rows. Push Ns from NWP to WP and make a hem by placing loops of first row worked in MC evenly along the row. Unravel WY when work is completed *.
1st size Inc 1 st at each end.
2nd size Inc 1 st at right edge.
All sizes 154 [168, 182] sts.
All machines
Set RC at 000. Using MT, K 1 row. Release card and cont in Fair Isle with MC in Feeder 1(A) and C in Feeder 2(B). K 18 rows. Shape sides by inc 1 st at each end of next and every foll 20th row until there are 166 [180, 194] sts. K 60 rows. RC shows 180 and work measures 48.5 cm, 19 in.
Shape armholes Cast off (bind off) 12 sts at beg of next 2 rows. 142 [156, 170] sts **.
K 106 rows.
Shape neck Note patt row on card.
Using a length of MC, cast off (bind off) centre 56 sts. Using nylon cord, K 43 [50, 57] sts at left by hand taking Ns down to NWP. Cont on rem sts for first side.
K 1 row. Dec 1 st at beg of next and foll alt row. 41 [48, 55] sts. K 2 rows. Cont in st st. K 2 rows in MC. Using WY, K a few rows and release from machine.
With carriage at right, unravel nylon cord over rem Ns, bringing Ns back to WP. Lock card on number previously noted. Take carriage to left without knitting. Release card and cont in Fair Isle. Finish to correspond with first side reversing shapings.

FRONT
Work as for Back to **.
K 86 rows.
Shape neck Note patt row on card.
Using a length of MC, cast off (bind off) centre 34 sts. Using nylon cord, K 54 [61, 68] sts at left by hand, taking Ns down to NWP. Cont on rem sts for first side.
K 1 row. Dec 1 st (3 sts in) at beg of next and

every foll alt row until 41 [48, 55] sts rem. Cont in st st. K 2 rows in MC. Using WY, K a few rows and release from machine.
With carriage at right, unravel nylon cord over rem Ns bringing Ns back to WP. Lock card on number previously noted. Take carriage to left without knitting. Release card and cont in Fair Isle. Finish to correspond with first side reversing shapings.

SLEEVES
Machines with ribber
With ribber in position and carriage at right, set machine for 1×1 rib. Push 28 Ns at left and right of centre 0 to WP. 56 Ns. Work as for Back from * to *.
Machines without ribber
Insert card and lock on first row. Push 28 Ns at left and right of centre 0 to WP. 56 Ns. Work as for Back from * to *.

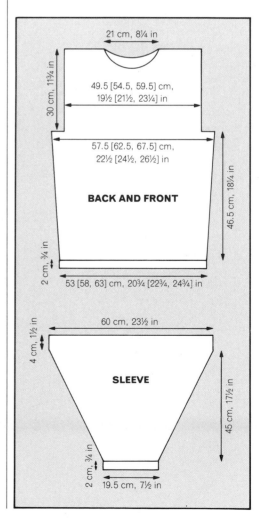

21 cm, 8¼ in
30 cm, 11¾ in
49.5 [54.5, 59.5] cm, 19½ [21½, 23¼] in
57.5 [62.5, 67.5] cm, 22½ [24½, 26½] in
BACK AND FRONT
46.5 cm, 18¼ in
2 cm, ¾ in
53 [58, 63] cm, 20¾ [22¾, 24¾] in

60 cm, 23½ in
4 cm, 1½ in
SLEEVE
45 cm, 17½ in
2 cm, ¾ in
19.5 cm, 7½ in

62

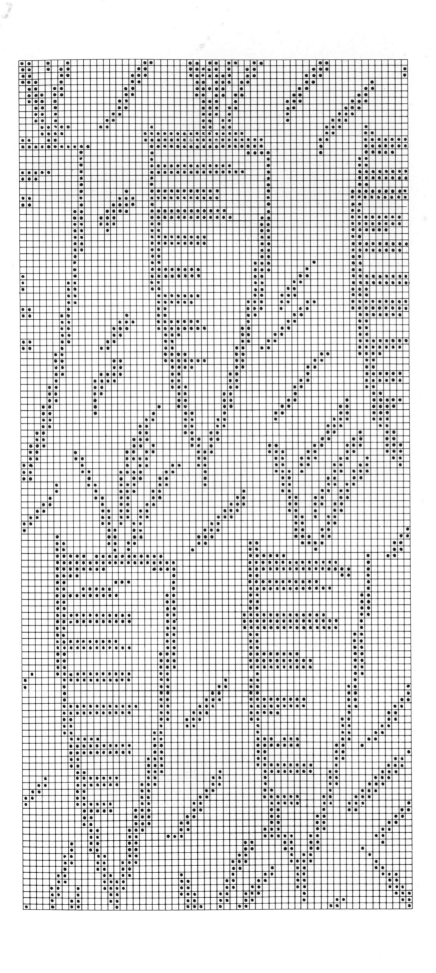

All machines
Set RC at 000. Using MT, K 1 row. Release card and cont in Fair Isle patt with MC in Feeder 1(A) and C in Feeder 2(B). K 1 row. Shape sides by inc 1 st at each end of next and every foll 3rd row until there are 124 sts, then on every foll alt row until there are 172 sts. K 25 rows. RC shows 175 and work measures 47 cm, 18½ in. Place marker at each end. K 14 rows. Cont in st st. K 2 rows in MC. Using WY, K a few rows and release from machine.

TO JOIN RIGHT SHOULDER
Push 41 [48, 55] Ns to WP. With K side of right back shoulder facing, replace 41 [48, 55] sts from last row worked in MC on to Ns. With P side of right front shoulder facing, replace 41 [48, 55] sts from last row worked in MC on to same Ns. Unravel WY. Using MT and MC, K 1 row. Cast off (bind off).

NECKBAND
Machines with ribber
With ribber in position and carriage at right, set machine for 1×1 rib. Using MC, cast on 140 sts in 1×1 rib. K 3 tubular rows. Carriage is at right. Set carriage for 1×1 rib knitting. Set RC at 000. Using MT-6/MT-6, K 24 rows. Transfer sts for st st. With P side facing, pick up 140 sts around neck edge and place on to Ns. Using MT and MC, K 1 row. Cast off (bind off).
Machines without ribber
Push 140 ns to WP. With K side facing, pick up 140 sts around neck edge and place on to Ns. Set RC at 000. Using MT-1 and MC, K 1 row. Transfer every 3rd st on to adjacent N and push empty Ns to NWP. Using MT-2, K 7 rows. Using MT-3, K 15 rows. Using MT-2, K 6 rows. Push Ns from NWP to WP and place loop from row below adjacent st on to empty Ns. Using MT-1, K 2 rows. Using WY, K a few rows and release from machine.

TO JOIN LEFT SHOULDER
Work as for right shoulder reading left for right.

TO JOIN SLEEVES TO ARMHOLES
Push 172 Ns to WP. With K side of sleeve facing, replace 172 sts on to Ns. With P side facing, pick up 172 sts along side edge of armhole and place on to same Ns. Using MT and MC, K 1 row. Cast off (bind off).

PRESSING
With wrong side facing, pin out all pieces to measurements given. Cover with a damp cloth and steam press.

MAKING UP
Join neckband, side and sleeve seams, sewing rows above markers to cast off (bound off) sts of armholes.
Machines without ribber Fold neckband in half to right side and pin in position. Unravelling WY as required, backstitch through open loops of last row worked in MC.

Windfall

This leaf motif cardigan has two handy pockets and a V-neck. The narrow front ribs are knitted in two pieces, joining at the centre back.

PATTERN RATING
● ● Fairly easy, for knitters with some experience.

MACHINES
This pattern is suitable for standard gauge punchcard machines.

MATERIALS
Rowan Fine Fleck Tweed.
130 g (5 oz) in shade 62 (MC).
290 g (10½ oz) in shade 51 (A).
120 g (4½ oz) in shade 1 (B).
4 buttons.
Rowan Fine Fleck Tweed is 75% Pure New Wool base, 15% Cotton Nepp, 10% Nylon.

YARN THICKNESS
Medium yarn.

MEASUREMENTS
To fit chest 87-97 cm, 34-38 in.
Actual measurement 113 cm, 44½ in.
Length to shoulder 50.5 cm, 20 in.
Sleeve seam 46 cm, 18¼ in.

TENSION
30 stitches and 39 rows to 10 cm, 4 in measured over Fair Isle pattern (tension dial setting approximately 7).
For perfect results, your tension must be matched exactly before starting the garment.

ABBREVIATIONS
See page 9.

NOTES
Knit side of knitting is right side of finished garment.
The card shown on page 65 should be punched, if required, before starting to knit.
Two colour Fair Isle rows should be knitted with the first colour given in the back feeder 1(A) to knit the background and the second colour given in the front feeder 2(B) to knit the contrast pattern.

FAIR ISLE PATTERN
K 15 rows A/B and 19 rows A/MC.

BACK
Machines with ribber
With ribber in position and carriage at right, set machine for 1×1 rib. Push 77 Ns at left

The alternating leaf motifs are knitted in two contrasting colours, the boldness of the design toned down by the tweed effect.

and right of centre 0 to WP. 154 Ns.
* Push corresponding Ns on ribber to WP. Arrange Ns for 1×1 rib. Using A, cast on and K 3 tubular rows. Carriage is at right. Set carriage for 1×1 rib knitting. Set RC at 000. Using MT-6/MT-6, K 14 rows. Transfer sts for st st *.
Machines without ribber
Push 76 Ns at left and right of centre 0 to WP. 152 Ns.
* Push every 3rd N back to NWP. Using MT and WY, cast on and K a few rows ending with carriage at left. Set RC at 000. Using MT-2 and A, K 27 rows. Push Ns from NWP to WP and make a hem by placing loops of first row worked in A evenly along the row. Unravel WY when work is completed *. Inc 1 st at each end. 154 sts.
All machines
Insert punchcard and lock on first row. Set carriage for patt. Set RC at 000. Using MT, K 1 row. Release card and cont in Fair Isle patt. K 6 rows. Shape sides by inc 1 st at each end of next and every foll 8th row until there are 172 sts. K 4 rows. RC shows 76

and work measures 22.5 cm, 9 in.
Shape armholes Cast off (bind off) 18 sts at beg of next 2 rows. 136 sts. K 102 rows.
Shape neck Note patt row on card. Using a length of A, cast off (bind off) centre 62 sts. Using nylon cord, K sts at left by hand taking Ns down to NWP. Cont on rem sts for first side.
K 1 row. Dec 1 st at beg of next and foll alt row. 35 sts. K 2 rows. Using WY, K a few rows in st st and release from machine. With carriage at right, unravel nylon cord over rem Ns bringing Ns back to WP. Lock card on number previously noted. Set carriage for patt and take to left without knitting. Release card and cont in Fair Isle patt. Finish to correspond with first side reversing shaping.

RIGHT FRONT
Machines with ribber
With ribber in position and carriage at right, set machine for 1×1 rib. Push Ns 4 to 77 inclusive at right of centre 0 to WP. 74 Ns. Work as for back from * to *.
Machines without ribber
Push Ns 4 to 77 inclusive at right of centre 0 to WP. 74 Ns. Work as for back from * to *.
All machines
** Insert punchcard and lock on first row. Set carriage for patt. Set RC at 000. Using MT, K 1 row. Release card and cont in Fair Isle patt. K 6 rows. Shape side by inc 1 st at right edge (left edge on left front) of next and every foll 8th row until there are 83 sts. K 4 rows. RC shows 76 and work measures 22.5 cm, 9 in. (K 1 row extra for left front only.)
Shape armhole Cast off (bind off) 18 sts at beg of next row. 65 sts. K 47 rows.
Shape front edge Dec 1 st at left edge (right edge on left front) of next and every foll alt row until 35 sts rem. K 3 rows (2 rows only on left front). RC shows 186 and work measures 50.5 cm, 20 in. Using WY, K a few rows in st st and release from machine **.

LEFT FRONT
Machines with ribber
With ribber in position and carriage at right, set machine for 1×1 rib. Push Ns 4 to 77 inclusive at left of centre 0 to WP. 74 Ns. Work as for back from * to *.
Machines without ribber
Push Ns 4 to 77 inclusive at left of centre 0 to WP. 74 Ns. Work as for back from * to *.

All machines

Work as for right front from ** to **
reversing shapings by noting alterations in
number of rows worked.

SLEEVES
Machines with ribber

With ribber in position and carriage at right,
set machine for 1×1 rib. Push 30 Ns at left
and right of centre 0 to WP. 60 Ns. Work as
for back to * to *.

Machines without ribber

Push 30 Ns at left and 29 Ns at right of
centre 0 to WP. 59 Ns. Work as for back
from * to *. Inc 1 st at right edge. 60 sts.

All machines

Insert punchcard and lock on 16th row. Set
carriage for patt. Set RC at 000. Using MT, K
1 row. Release card and cont in Fair Isle patt
(starting with 16th row). K 1 row. Shape
sides by inc 1 st at each end of next and
every foll 3rd row until there are 168 sts. K 6
rows. RC shows 168 and work measures 46
cm, 18¼ in. Place marker at each end. K 22
rows. Cont in st st and A, K 2 rows. Using
WY, K a few rows and release from
machine.

RIGHT POCKET

Push Ns 16 to 49 inclusive at right of centre
0 to WP. 34 Ns. Using MT and WY, cast on
and K a few rows ending with carriage at
left. Insert punchcard and lock on first row.
Set carriage for patt. Set RC at 000. Using
A, K 1 row. Release card and cont in Fair
Isle patt. K 34 rows. Cont in st st and A, K 1
row. Using WY, K a few rows and release
from machine.

LEFT POCKET

Work as for right pocket reversing shapings
by reading left for right and right for left.

POCKET TOPS
Machines with ribber

With ribber in position and carriage at right,
set machine for 1×1 rib. Using A, cast on 34
sts in 1×1 rib. K 3 tubular rows. Carriage is
at right. Set carriage for 1×1 rib knitting. Set
RC at 000. Using MT-6/MT-6, K 7 rows.
Transfer sts for st st.

Machines without ribber

Push 35 Ns to WP. Push every 3rd N back to
NWP. Using MY and WY, cast on and K a
few rows ending with carriage at left. Set RC
at 000. Using MT-2 and A, K 13 rows. Push
Ns from NWP to WP and make a hem by
placing loops of first row worked in A evenly
along the row. Unravel WY when work is
completed. Dec 1 st. 34 sts.

All machines

With P side facing, replace sts from last row
of pocket on to Ns. Using MT, K 1 row. Cast
off (bind off).

BUTTONHOLE BAND
Machines with ribber

With ribber in position and carriage at right,
set machine for 1×1 rib. Using A, cast on

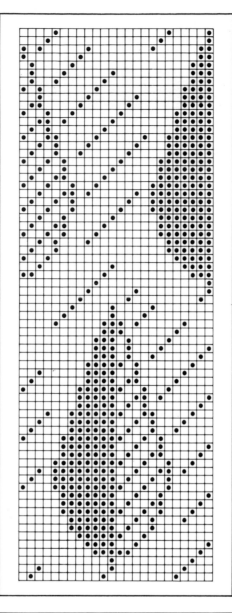

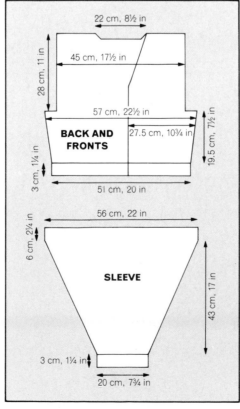

22 cm, 8½ in

45 cm, 17½ in

28 cm, 11 in

57 cm, 22½ in

BACK AND FRONTS   27.5 cm, 10¾ in

19.5 cm, 7½ in

3 cm, 1¼ in

51 cm, 20 in

56 cm, 22 in

6 cm, 2¼ in

SLEEVE

43 cm, 17 in

3 cm, 1¼ in

20 cm, 7¾ in

170 sts in 1×1 rib. K 3 tubular rows. Carriage
is at right. Set carriage for 1×1 rib knitting.
Set RC at 000. Using MT-6/MT-6, K 7 rows.
Counting from right edge, make buttonholes
over sts 5, 6; 35, 36; 65, 66; 95 and 96. K 15
rows. Make buttonholes over same sts as
before. K 7 rows. Transfer sts for st st.
Using WY, K a few rows and release from
machine.

Machines without ribber

Push 170 Ns to WP. Using MT and WY, cast
on and K a few rows ending with carriage at
left. Set RC at 000. Using MT-1 and A, K 6
rows. Counting from right edge, make
buttonholes over sts 5, 6; 35, 36; 65, 66; 95
and 96. K 13 rows. Make buttonholes over
same sts as before. K 6 rows. Make a hem
by placing loops of first row worked in A on
to corresponding Ns. Unravel WY when
work is completed. K 1 row. Using WY, K a
few rows and release from machine.

BUTTON BAND

Work as for buttonhole band omitting
buttonholes.

TO JOIN RIGHT SHOULDER

Push 35 Ns to WP. With K side of right back
shoulder facing, replace sts on to Ns.
Unravel WY. With P side of right front
shoulder facing, replace sts on to same Ns.
Unravel WY. Using MT and A, K 1 row. Cast
off (bind off).

TO JOIN LEFT SHOULDER

Work as for right shoulder, reading left for
right.

TO JOIN SLEEVES AND ARMHOLES

Push 168 Ns to WP. With K side of sleeve
facing, replace 168 sts on to Ns. Unravel
WY. With P side facing, pick up 168 sts
along side of armhole and place on to same
Ns. Using MT and A, K 1 row. Cast off
(bind off).

PRESSING

With wrong side facing, pin out all pieces to
measurements given. Press carefully
following instructions on cone band.

MAKING UP

Sew rows above markers on sleeves to cast
off (bound off) sts on back and fronts. Join
side and sleeve seams. Sew pockets into
position. Join ends of front bands.

Machines with ribber

Pin front bands into position, with
buttonholes on right or left front. Unravelling
WY as required, backstitch through open
loops of last row worked in A. Fold in half to
inside and slipstitch down.

Machines without ribber

Pin front bands into position with
buttonholes on right or left front. Unravelling
WY as required, backstitch through open
loops of last row worked in A.

All machines

Finish buttonholes and sew on buttons.

65

Windfall Dress

A simple dress slightly shaped at the waist, with
turnover collar and deep armholes narrowing to cuffs.

PATTERN RATING
●● Fairly easy, for knitters with some
experience.

MACHINES
This pattern is suitable for standard gauge
punchcard machines.

MATERIALS
Rowan Fine Fleck Tweed.
490 g in shade 62 (MC).
*Rowan Fine Fleck Tweed is 75% Pure New
Wool base, 15% Cotton Nepp, 10% Nylon.*

YARN THICKNESS
Medium yarn.

MEASUREMENTS
To fit chest 87-97 cm, 34-38 in.
Actual measurement 104 cm, 41 in.
Length to shoulder 91.5 cm, 36 in.
Sleeve seam 49.5 cm, 19½ in.

TENSION
27 stitches and 39 rows to 10 cm, 4 in
measured over stocking stitch (tension dial
setting approximately 7).
*For perfect results, your tension must be
matched exactly before starting the
garment.*

ABBREVIATIONS
See page 9.

NOTES
Knit side of knitting is right side of finished
garment.

BACK
Machines with ribber
With ribber in position and carriage at right,
set machine for 1×1 rib. Using MC, cast on
142 sts in 1×1 rib. K 3 tubular rows. Carriage
is at right. Set carriage for 1×1 rib knitting.
Set RC at 000. Using MT-6/MT-6, K 14 rows.
Transfer sts for st st.
Machines without ribber
Push 140 Ns to WP. Push every 3rd N back
to NWP. Using MT and WY, cast on and K a
few rows ending with carriage at left. Set RC
at 000. Using MT-2 and MC, K 27 rows. Push
Ns from NWP to WP and make a hem by
placing loops of first row worked in MC
evenly along the row. Unravel WY when work
is completed. Inc 1 st at each end. 142 sts.

All machines
Set RC at 000. Using MT, K 111 rows. Shape
sides by dec 1 st (3 sts in) at each end of
next and every foll 6th row until 118 sts rem.
RC shows 178 and work measures 48.5 cm,
19 in. K 11 rows. Inc 1 st (3 sts in) at each
end of next and every foll 5th row until there
are 142 sts. K 3 rows. RC shows 248 and
work measures 66.5 cm, 26¼ in.
Shape armholes Cast off (bind off) 10 sts at
beg of next 2 rows. 122 sts. *.
K 90 rows.

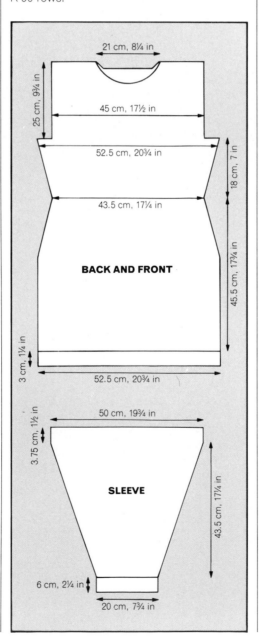

21 cm, 8¼ in

25 cm, 9¾ in

45 cm, 17½ in

52.5 cm, 20¾ in

43.5 cm, 17¼ in

18 cm, 7 in

BACK AND FRONT

45.5 cm, 17¾ in

3 cm, 1¼ in

52.5 cm, 20¾ in

3.75 cm, 1½ in

50 cm, 19¾ in

SLEEVE

43.5 cm, 17¼ in

6 cm, 2¼ in

20 cm, 7¾ in

Shape neck Using a length of MC, cast off
(bind off) centre 54 sts. Push Ns at left to HP
and cont on rem sts for first side.
K 1 row. Dec 1 st at beg of next and foll alt
row. 32 sts, K 2 rows. Using WY, K a few
rows and release from machine. With
carriage at left, push rem Ns from HP to
UWP. Finish to correspond with first side
reversing shapings.

FRONT
Work as for back to *.
K 68 rows.
Shape neck Using a length of MC, cast off
(bind off) centre 34 sts. Push Ns at left to HP
and cont on rem sts for first side.
K 1 row. Dec 1 st at beg of next and every foll
alt row until 32 sts rem. K 4 rows. Using
WY, K a few rows and release from
machine.
With carriage at left, push rem Ns from HP
to UWP. Finish to correspond with first side
reversing shapings.

SLEEVES
Machines with ribber
With ribber in position and carriage at right,
set machine for 1×1 rib. Using MC, cast on
54 sts in 1×1 rib. K 3 tubular rows. Carriage
is at right. Set carriage for 1×1 rib knitting.
Set RC at 000. Using MT-6/MT-6, K 30 rows.
Transfer sts for st st.
Machines without ribber
Push 53 Ns to WP. Push every 3rd N back to
NWP. Using MT and WY, cast on and K a
few rows ending with carriage at left. Set RC
at 000. Using MT-2 and MC, K 55 rows.
Push Ns from NWP to WP and make a hem
by placing loops of first row worked in MC
evenly along the row. Unravel WY when
work is completed. Inc 1 st. 54 sts.
All machines
Set RC at 000. Using MT, K 2 rows. Shape
sides by inc 1 st (3 sts in) at each end of next
and every foll 3rd row until there are 136 sts.
K 47 rows. RC shows 170 and work
measures 49.5 cm, 19½ in. Place marker at
each end. K 14 rows. Using WY, K a few
rows and release from machine.

TO JOIN RIGHT SHOULDER
Push 32 Ns to WP. With K side of right back
shoulder facing, replace sts on to Ns.
Unravel WY. With P side of right front
shoulder facing, replace sts on to same Ns.

Unravel WY. Using MT and MC, K 1 row. Cast off (bind off).

COLLAR

Machines with ribber

With ribber in position and carriage at right, set machine for full needle rib/double rib. Push 145 Ns to WP on both beds for full needle rib/double rib. Using MC, cast on and K 3 tubular rows. Carriage is at right. Set carriage for full needle rib/double rib knitting. Set RC at 000. Using MT-6/MT-6, K 50 rows. Transfer sts for st st. With P side facing, pick up 145 sts around neck edge and place on to Ns. Using MT, K 1 row. Cast off (bind off).

Machines without ribber

Push 146 Ns to WP. Push every 3rd N back to NWP. Using MT and WY, cast on and K a few rows ending with carriage at left. Set RC at 000. Using MT-2 and MC, K 21 rows. Using MT-1, K 47 rows. Using MT-2, K 21 rows. Push Ns from NWP to WP and make a hem by placing loops of first row worked in MC evenly along the row. Unravel WY when work is completed. Using MT, K 2 rows. Using WY, K a few rows and release from machine.

TO JOIN LEFT SHOULDER

Work as for right shoulder, reading left for right.

TO JOIN SLEEVES AND ARMHOLES

Push 136 Ns to WP. With K side of sleeve facing, replace sts on to Ns. Unravel WY. With P side facing, pick up sts along side of armhole and place on to same Ns. Using MT and MC, K 1 row. Cast off (bind off).

PRESSING

With wrong side facing, pin out all pieces to measurements given. Press carefully following instructions on cone band.

MAKING UP

Sew rows above markers on sleeves to cast off (bound off) sts on back and front. Join side, collar and sleeve seams.

Machines without ribber

Pin collar into position. Unravelling WY as required, backstitch through open loops of last row worked in MC.

Ethnographic

These designs were inspired by my travels in India – although, apart from the Lotus design derived from tiles in a Maharajah's palace in Udaipur, Rajasthan, they seem to have a more Latin American feel. Museums, galleries, and books on various textile crafts provide a huge variety of design reference if you want to create your own designs.

The patterns, although they look at first like regular geometric repeats, are actually irregular, creating an earthy, more peasanty and individual style. Because of the fairly large pattern repeats, you may need to tack up the floats on the back of the fabric on the sleeves, although it probably isn't necessary on the body pieces.

The Block Print echoes the traditional appliqué technique of sewing scraps of coloured cotton squares onto woven cloth. This sweater is a conventional shape with a comfortable crew neck and deep armholes. It is most successful if you keep the ground colour neutral (black or cream) or, as it's knitted here, in a donkey grey. Almost any colour can be used for the Fair Isle, though I would suggest repeating some of the colours, to give the design an overall cohesion. The scale of this pattern can be successfully reduced if you wished to adapt the design for a child's sweater.

The Rough Diamond is derived from a Rajasthani tile design and looks very different if you experiment with the background colours, keeping them fairly neutral. The colour sequence is relatively complicated, so it's a good idea to knit up a long swatch if you do change the colours around. The dress can be worn belted or straight and the length can be altered by omitting a sequence of the diamond repeat. For spring, the cardigan could be knitted in cotton with paler background colours and cooler pattern colours.

Braided Zigzag can be worn as a dress or as an oversized sweater, belted or straight. I've knitted it here with changing bands of colour, but you could use just one colour, i.e. repeating the sequence of the black band.

The Child's Lotus is a reverse colourway of the Man's Lotus and dramatically illustrates the effect of playing around with colours. If you're going to design your own colourways, it's quite important to knit the full pattern repeat first. Once you are satisfied with the swatch, you can always unravel the knitting and re-use the yarn. Alternatively, when you've knitted a collection of swatches for different designs, sew them together to make an interesting if slightly eccentric blanket!

Braided Zigzag

Can be worn as a dress or oversized sweater, belted or straight.
You could alter the length by omitting a zigzag repeat.

PATTERN RATING
● ● ● ● Recommended for experts only.

MACHINES
This pattern is suitable for standard gauge punchcard machines.

MATERIALS
Rowan Botany Wool.
340 g (12 oz) in shade 84 (A).
200 g (7 oz) in shade 60 (B).
120 g (4½ oz) in shade 62 (C).
90 g (3½ oz) in shade 45 (D).
40 g (1½ oz) in shade 9 (E).
Rowan Botany Wool is 100% Pure New Wool.

YARN THICKNESS
Medium yarn.

MEASUREMENTS
To fit chest 87-97 cm, 34-38 in.
Actual measurement 121 cm, 47½ in.
Length to shoulder 86.5 cm, 34 in.
Sleeve seam 48.5 cm, 19¼ in.

TENSION
32 stitches and 40 rows to 10 cm, 4 in.
measured over Fair Isle pattern (tension dial
setting approximately 7).
*For perfect results, your tension must be
matched exactly before starting the
garment.*

ABBREVIATIONS
See page 9.

NOTE
Knit side of knitting is right side of finished
garment.
The card shown on this page should be
punched, if required, before starting to knit.
Two colour Fair Isle rows should be knitted
with the first colour given in the back feeder
1(A) to knit the background and the second
colour given in the front feeder 2(B) to knit
the contrast pattern.

FAIR ISLE PATTERN
K 17 rows A/D, 2 rows A only (st st), 5 rows
A/C, 4 rows A/B, 5 rows B/E, 18 rows A/B, 5
rows B/E, 4 rows A/B, 5 rows A/C, 2 rows A
only (st st), 17 rows A/B, 2 rows A only (st
st), 5 rows A/D, 4 rows A/C, 5 rows C/E, 18
rows A/C, 5 rows C/E, 4 rows A/C, 5 rows
A/D, 2 rows A only (st st), 17 rows A/C, 2

rows A only (st st), 5 rows A/B, 4 rows A/D,
5 rows D/E, 18 rows A/D, 5 rows D/E, 4 rows
A/D, 5 rows A/B and 2 rows A only (st st).
These 201 rows form patt.

BACK
Machines with ribber
With ribber in position and carriage at right,
sert machine for 1×1 rib. Push 87 Ns at left
and right of centre 0 to WP. 174 Ns.
* Push corresponding Ns on ribber to WP.
Arrange Ns for 1×1 rib. Using B, cast on
and K 3 tubular rows. Carriage is at right.
Set carriage for 1×1 rib knitting. Set RC at
000. Using MT-6/MT-6, K 14 rows. Transfer
sts for st st *.
Machines without ribber
Push 87 Ns at left and 86 Ns at right of
centre 0 to WP. 173 Ns.
* Push every 3rd N back to NWP. Using MT
and WY, cast on and K a few rows ending
with carriage at left. Set RC at 000. Using
MT-4 and B, K 25 rows. Push Ns from NWP
to WP and make a hem by placing loops of
first row rorked in B evenly along the row.
Unravel WY when work is completed *.
Inc 1 st at right edge. 174 sts.

All machines
Insert punchcard and lock on first row. Set
carriage for patt. Set RC at 000. Using MT
and A, K 1 row. Release card and cont in
Fair Isle patt. K 18 rows. Shape sides by inc 1
st at each end of next and every foll 20th row
until there are 196 sts. K 12 rows. RC shows
232 and work measures 60.5 cm, 23¾ in.
Place marker at each end **.
K 98 rows.
Shape neck Note patt row on card. Using a
length of A, cast off (bind off) centre 68 sts.
Using nylon cord, K 64 sts at left by hand
taking Ns down to NWP. Cont on rem sts for
first side.
K 1 row. Dec 1 st at beg of next and foll alt
row. 62 sts. Cont in st st and A. K 2 rows.
Using WY, K a few rows and release from
machine.
With carriage at right, unravel nylon cord
over rem Ns bringing Ns back to WP. Lock
card on number previously noted. Take
carriage to left without knitting. Release
card and cont in Fair Isle patt. Finish to
correspond with first side reversing shapings.

FRONT
Work as for back to **. K 84 rows.

Shape neck Note patt row on card. Using a
length of C, cast off (bind off) centre 54 sts.
Using nylon cord, K 71 sts at left by hand
taking Ns down to NWP. Cont on rem sts for
first side.
K 1 row. Dec 1 st at beg of next and every foll
alt row until 62 sts rem. Cont in st st and A.
K 2 rows. Using WY, K a few rows and
release from machine.
With carriage at right, unravel nylon cord
over rem Ns bringing Ns back to WP. Lock
card on number previously noted. Take

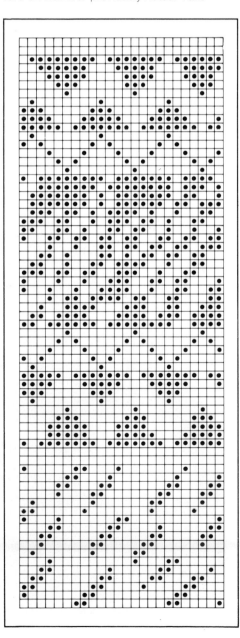

carriage to left without knitting. Release card and cont in Fair Isle patt. Finish to correspond with first side reversing shapings.

SLEEVES

Machines with ribber
With ribber in position and carriage at right, set machine for 1×1 rib. Push 38 Ns at left and right of centre 0 to WP. 76 Ns. Work as for back from * to *.

Machines without ribber
Push 37 Ns at left and right of centre 0 to WP. 74 Ns. Work as for back from * to *. Inc 1 st at each end. 76 sts.

74 All machines
Set RC at 000. Using MT and A, K 1 row. Insert punchcard and lock on 20th row. Set carriage for patt. Shape sides by inc 1 st at each end of next row. Release card and cont in Fair Isle patt (starting with row 20). Inc 1 st at each end of every foll 4th row from previous inc until there are 168 sts. Cont in st st and A. K 2 rows. RC shows 184 and work measures 48.5 cm, 19¼ in. Using WY, K a few rows and release from machine.

COLLAR

Machines with ribber
With ribber in position and carriage at right,

set machine for full needle rib/double rib. Push 140 Ns on both beds to WP for full needle rib/double rib. Using B, cast on and K 3 tubular rows. Carriage is at right. Set carriage for full needle rib/double rib knitting. Set RC at 000. Using MT-4/MT-4, K 50 rows. Transfer sts to main bed. Cast off (bind off).

Machines without ribber
Push 179 Ns to WP. Push every 3rd N back to NWP. Using MT and WY, cast on and K a few rows ending with carriage at left. Set RC at 000. Using MT-4 and B, K 24 rows. Using MT-3, K 51 rows. Using MT-4, K 24 rows. Push Ns from NWP to WP and make a hem by placing loops of first row worked in B evenly along the row. Unravel WY when work is completed. Using MT, K 2 rows. Using WY, K a few rows and release from machine.

TO JOIN RIGHT SHOULDER
Push 62 Ns to WP.
With K side of right back shoulder facing, replace sts on to Ns.
Unravel WY. With P side of right front shoulder facing, replace sts on to same Ns. Unravel WY. Using MT and A, K 1 row. Cast off (bind off).

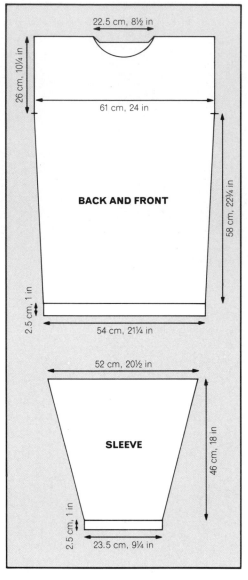

TO JOIN LEFT SHOULDER
Work as for right shoulder but read left for right.

TO JOIN SLEEVES TO ARMHOLES
Push 168 Ns to WP. With K side facing, replace 168 sts from top of sleeve on to Ns. Unravel WY. With P side facing, pick up 168 sts between markers and place on to same Ns. Using MT and A, K 1 row. Cast off (bind off).

PRESSING
With wrong side facing, pin out pieces to measurements given. Press carefully following instructions on cone band.

MAKING UP
Join side, sleeve and collar seams.
Machines with ribber
Sew cast off (bound off) edge of collar into position with seam at centre back.
Machines without ribber
Pin collar into position with seam at centre back. Unravelling WY as required, backstitch through open loops of last row worked in B.
All machines
Fold collar in half to right side.

Block Print

Traditional shape with an unconventional
pattern, comfortable crew neck and armholes. This design is
most successful with a neutral background.

PATTERN RATING
● ● ● For fairly experienced knitters.

MACHINES
This pattern is suitable for electronic
machines.

MATERIALS
Rowan Botany Wool.
325 g (12 oz) in shade 635 (A).
60 g (2 oz) in shade 62 (B).
75 g (3 oz) in shade 45 (C).
40 g (1½ oz) in shade 9 (D).
130 g (5 oz) in shade 614 (E).
Rowan Botany Wool is 100% Pure New Wool.

YARN THICKNESS
Medium yarn.

MEASUREMENTS
To fit chest 92-97 [102-107, 112-117] cm, 36-38
[40-42, 44-46] in.
Actual size 103 [112, 122] cm, 40½ [44, 48] in.
Length to shoulder 65.5 cm, 25¾ in.
Sleeve seam 51.5 cm, 20¼ in.
*Instructions are written for the smallest size,
larger sizes follow in square brackets. If only
one figure is given, it applies to all sizes.*

TENSION
31 stitches and 40 rows to 10 cm, 4 in
measured over Fair Isle pattern (tension dial
setting approximately 7).
*For perfect results, your tension must be
matched exactly before starting the
garment.*

ABBREVIATIONS
See page 9.

NOTES
Knit side of knitting is right side of finished
garment. Fill in the pattern cards on pages
76 and 77, if required, before starting to knit.
Centre pattern on machine.
Knitmaster machines
Place needle 1 cam between Ns 30 and 31 to
centre patt. Press button 2 (right light on) to
reverse direction of pattern.
All machines
Two colour Fair Isle rows should be knitted
with the first colour given in the back feeder
1(A) to knit the background and the second
colour given in the front feeder 2(B) to knit
the contrast pattern.

FAIR ISLE PATTERN
K 15 rows A/B. Lock card. Cont in st st. K 2
rows E, 2 rows D, 14 rows C, 2 rows D, 2
rows E and 1 row A. Release card and cont
in Fair Isle. K 1 row A only (st st), 6 rows A/E,
2 rows A only (st st), 12 rows A/C, 2 rows A
only (st st), 19 rows A/B, 2 rows A only (st
st), 6 rows A/D, 2 rows A only (st st), 36
rows A/E, 4 rows A only (st st), 15 rows A/D,
2 rows A only (st st), 9 rows A/B and 1 row A
only (st st). Remove card. Insert card 2 and
lock on first row. K 1 row A only (st st).
Release card. K 23 rows A/C, 2 rows A only
(st st), 15 rows A/E, 5 rows A only (st st), 6
rows A/B, 4 rows A only (st st), 20 rows A/D,
5 rows A only (st st) and 11 rows A/C.

BACK
Machines with ribber
With ribber in position and carriage at right,
set machine for 1×1 rib. Push 73 [80, 88] Ns
at left and right of centre 0 to WP. 146 [160,
176] Ns.
* Push corresponding Ns on ribber to WP.
Arrange Ns for next 1×1 rib. Using A, cast
on and K 3 tubular rows. Carriage is at
right. Set carriage for 1×1 rib knitting. Insert
card 1 and lock on first row. Set RC at 000.
Using MT-6/MT-6, K 14 rows. Transfer sts for
st st *.
Machines without ribber
Push 73 [79, 88] Ns at left and right of centre
0 to WP. 146 [158, 176] Ns.

* Push every 3rd N back to NWP. Using MT and WY, cast on and K a few rows ending with carriage at left. Insert card 1 and lock on first row. Set RC at 000. Using MT-4 and A, K 25 rows. Push Ns from NWP to WP and make a hem by placing loops of first row worked in A evenly along the row. Unravel WY when work is completed *.

2nd size Inc 1 st at each end.

All sizes 146 [160, 176] sts.

All machines

Set RC at 000. Using MT, K 1 row. Release card and cont in Fair Isle patt. K 13 rows. Shape sides by inc 1 st at each end of next and every foll 15th row until there are 162 [176, 192] sts. K 20 rows. RC shows 140 and work measures 37.5 cm, 14¾ in.

Shape armholes Cast off (bind off) 15 sts at beg of next 2 rows. 132 [146, 162] sts **.
K 104 rows.

Shape neck Note patt row on card. Using a length of A, cast off (bind off) centre 58 sts. Using nylon cord, K 37 [44, 52] sts at left by hand taking Ns down to NWP. Cont on rem sts for first side.

K 1 row. Dec 1 st at beg of next and foll alt row. 35 [42, 50] sts. Cont in st st and A. K 2 rows. Using WY, K a few rows and release from machine.

With carriage at right, unravel nylon cord over rem Ns bringing Ns back to WP. Lock card on number previously noted. Take carriage to left without knitting. Release card and cont in Fair Isle patt. Finish to correspond with first side reversing shapings.

FRONT

Work as for back to **.

K 82 rows.

Shape neck Note patt row on card. Using a length of A, cast off (bind off) centre 36 sts. Using nylon cord, K 48 [55, 63] sts at left by hand taking Ns down to NWP. Cont on rem sts for first side.

K 1 row. Dec 1 st (2 sts in) at beg of next and every foll alt row until 35 [42, 50] sts rem. Cont in st st and A, K 2 rows. Using WY, K a few rows and release from machine.

With carriage at right, unravel nylon cord over rem Ns bringing Ns back to WP. Lock card on number previously noted. Take carriage to left without knitting. Release card and cont in Fair Isle patt. Finish to correspond with first side reversing shapings.

SLEEVES

Machines with ribber

With ribber in position and carriage at right, set machine for 1×1 rib. Push 39 Ns at left and right of centre 0 to WP. 78 Ns. Work as for back from * to *.

Machines without ribber

Push 39 Ns at left and 38 Ns at right of centre 0 to WP. 77 Ns. Work as for back from * to *. Inc 1 st at right edge. 78 sts.

All machines

Set RC at 000. Using MT, K 1 row. Release card and cont in Fair Isle patt. K 2 rows. Shape sides by inc 1 st at each end of next

CARD 1

and every foll 4th row until there are 174 sts. K 5 rows. RC shows 197 and work measures 51.5 cm, 20¼ in. Place marker at each end. K 17 rows. Cont in st st and A. K 2 rows. Using WY, K a few rows and release from machine.

TO JOIN RIGHT SHOULDER
Push 35 [42, 50] Ns to WP. With K side of right back shoulder facing, replace sts on to Ns. Unravel WY. With P side of right front shoulder facing, replace sts on to same Ns. Unravel WY. Using MT and A, K 1 row. Cast off (bind off).

77

NECKBAND
Machines with ribber
With ribber in position and carriage at right, set machine for 1×1 rib. Using A, cast on 150 sts in 1×1 rib. K 3 tubular rows. Carriage is at right. Set carriage for 1×1 rib knitting. Set RC at 000. Using MT-6/MT-6, K 30 rows. Transfer sts for st st. Using WY, K a few rows and release from machine.

Machines without ribber
Push 152 Ns to WP. With K side facing, pick up sts around neck edge and place on to Ns. Set RC at 000. Using MT and A, K 1 row. Transfer every 3rd st on to adjacent N and push empty Ns to NWP. Using MT-3, K 6 rows. Using MT-4, K 13 rows. Using MT-3, K 5 rows. Push Ns from NWP to WP and place loop from row below adjacent st on to empty Ns. Using MT, K 2 rows. Using WY, K a few rows and release from machine.

TO JOIN LEFT SHOULDER
Work as for right shoulder but read left for right.

TO JOIN SLEEVES TO ARMHOLES
Push 174 Ns to WP. With K side facing, replace 174 sts from top of sleeve on to Ns. Unravel WY. With P side facing, pick up 174 sts along side edge of armhole and place on to same Ns. Using MT and A, K 1 row. Cast off (bind off).

PRESSING
With wrong side facing, pin out pieces to measurements given. Press carefully following instructions on cone band.

MAKING UP
Sew rows above markers on sleeves to cast off (bound off) sts on back and front. Join side and sleeve seams.
Machines with ribber
Join neckband seam. Pin neckband into position.
Unravelling WY as required, backstitch through open loops of last row worked in A. Fold in half to wrong side and slipstitch loosely in position.
Machines without ribber
Join neckband seam. Fold in half to right side and pin in position. Unravelling WY as required, backstitch through open loops of last row worked in A.

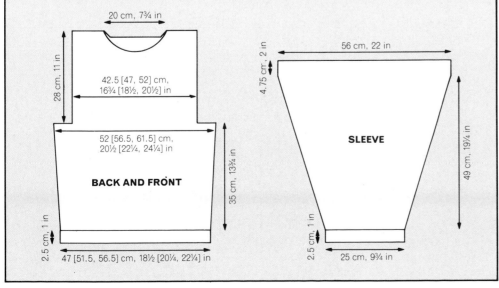

This design is derived from the lotus flower. Keeping the background neutral, you could use alternative colours in the patterning.

78 PATTERN RATING
● ● ● ● Recommended for experts only.

MACHINES
This pattern is suitable for standard gauge punchcard machines.

MATERIALS
Rowan Botany Wool.
310 g (11 oz) in shade 614 (A).
120 g (4½ oz) in shade 67 (B).
50 g (2 oz) in shade 45 (C).
40 g (1½ oz) in shade 108 (D).
40 g (1½ oz) in shade 9 (E).
Rowan Botany Wool is 100% Pure New Wool.

YARN THICKNESS
Medium yarn.

MEASUREMENTS
To fit chest 87-102 cm, 34-40 in.
Actual measurement 115 cm, 45¼ in.
Length to shoulder 69 cm, 27¼ in.
Sleeve seam 44 cm, 17¼ in.

TENSION
32 stitches and 40 rows to 10 cm, 4 in measured over Fair Isle pattern (tension dial setting approximately 7).
For perfect results, your tension must be matched exactly before starting the garment.

ABBREVIATIONS
See page 9.

NOTE
Knit side of knitting is right side of finished garment. The card shown on page 80 should be punched, if required, before starting to knit. Two colour Fair Isle rows should be knitted with the first colour given in the back feeder 1(A) to knit the background and the second colour given in the front feeder 2(B) to knit the contrast pattern.

FAIR ISLE PATTERN
K 4 rows A/B.
* 1 row A only (st st), 2 rows E/B, 1 row A only (st st), 4 rows A/B. 22 rows A/C, 1 row A only (st st), 2 rows A/E, 4 rows A/B, 1 row A only (st st), 2 rows E/B, 1 row A only (st st), 28 rows A/B, 1 row A only (st st), 2 rows C/B, 1 row A only (st st), 4 rows A/B, 22 rows A/D, 1 row A only (st st). 2 rows A/C, 4 rows A/B, 1 row A only (st st), 2 rows C/B, 1 row A only (st st), 28 rows A/B, 1 row A only (st st), 2 rows D/B, 1 row A only (st st), 4 rows A/B, 22 rows A/E, 1 row A only (st st), 2 rows A/D, 4 rows A/B, 1 row A only (st st), 2 rows D/B, 1 row A only (st st) and 28 rows A/B. These 207 rows from * form patt.

BACK
Machines with ribber
With ribber in position and carriage at right,

set machine for 1×1 rib. Push 85 Ns at left and right of centre 0 to WP. 170 Ns.
* Push corresponding Ns on ribber to WP. Arrange Ns for 1×1 rib. Using A, cast on and K 3 tubular rows. Carriage is at right. Set carriage for 1×1 rib knitting. Set RC at 000. Using MT-6/MT-6, K 14 rows. Transfer sts for st st *.

Machines without ribber
Push 85 Ns at left and right of centre 0 to WP. 170 Ns.
* Push every 3rd N back to NWP. Using MT and WY, cast on and K a few rows ending with carriage at left. Set RC at 000. Using MT-4 and A, K 25 rows. Push Ns from NWP to WP and make a hem by placing loops of first row worked in A evenly along the row. Unravel WY when work is completed *.

All machines
Insert punchcard and lock on first row. Set carriage for patt. Set RC at 000. Using MT, K 1 row. Release card and cont in Fair Isle patt. K 14 rows. Shape sides by inc 1 st at each end of next and every foll 16th row until there are 186 sts. K 22 rows. RC shows 150 and work measures 40 cm, 15¾ in.
Shape armholes Cast off (bind off) 18 sts at beg of next 2 rows. 150 sts **.
K 108 rows.
Shape neck Note patt row on card. Using a length of A, cast off (bind off) centre 66 sts. Using nylon cord, K 42 sts at left by hand taking Ns down to NWP. Cont on rem sts for first side.
K 1 row. Dec 1 st at beg of next and foll alt row. 40 sts. Cont in st st and A, K 2 rows. Using WY, K a few rows and release from machine.
With carriage at right, unravel nylon cord over rem Ns bringing Ns back to WP. Lock card on number previously noted. Take carriage to left without knitting. Release card and cont in Fair Isle patt. Finish to correspond with first side reversing shapings.

FRONT
Work as for back to **.
K 90 rows.
Shape neck Note patt row on card. Using a length of A, cast off (bind off) centre 48 sts. Using nylon cord, K 51 sts at left by hand taking Ns down to NWP. Cont on rem sts for first side.
K 1 row. Dec 1 st at beg of next and every foll alt row until 40 sts rem. Cont in st st and A,

---

BACK AND FRONT
21.5 cm, 8¼ in
29 cm, 11¼ in
46.5 cm, 18¼ in
58 cm, 22¾ in
37.5 cm, 14¾ in
2.5 cm, 1 in
53 cm, 20¾ in

SLEEVE
5.75 cm, 2¼ in
58 cm, 22¾ in
41.5 cm, 16¼ in
2.5 cm, 1 in
23.5 cm, 9¼ in

K 2 rows. Using WY, K a few rows and release from machine.

With carriage at right, unravel nylon cord over rem Ns bringing Ns back to WP. Lock card on number previously noted. Take carriage to left without knitting. Release card and cont in Fair Isle patt. Finish to correspond with first side reversing shapings.

SLEEVES

Machines with ribber

With ribber in position and carriage at right, set machine for 1×1 rib. Push 38 Ns at left and right of centre 0 to WP. 76 Ns. Work as for back from * to *.

Machines without ribber

Push 37 Ns at left and right of centre 0 to WP. 74 Ns. Work as for back from * to *. Inc 1 st at each end. 76 sts.

All machines

Insert punchcard and lock on first row. Set carriage for patt. Set RC at 000. Using MT, K 1 row. Release card and cont in Fair Isle patt. K 1 row. Shape sides by inc 1 st at each end of next and every foll 3rd row until there are 186 sts. K 2 rows. RC shows 167 and work measures 44 cm, 17¼ in. Place marker at each end. K 21 rows. Cont in st st and A, K 2 rows. Using WY, K a few rows and release from machine.

TO JOIN RIGHT SHOULDER

Push 40 Ns to WP. With K side of right back shoulder facing, replace sts on to Ns. Unravel WY. With P side of right front shoulder facing, replace sts on to same Ns. Unravel WY. Using MT and A, K 1 row. Cast off (bind off).

NECKBAND

Machines with ribber

With ribber in position and carriage at right, set machine for 1×1 rib. Using A, cast on 160 sts in 1×1 rib. K 3 tubular rows. Carriage is at right. Set carriage for 1×1 rib knitting. Set RC at 000. Using MT-6/MT-6, K 28 rows. Transfer sts for st st. Using WY, K a few rows and release from machine.

Machines without ribber

Push 161 Ns to WP. With K side facing, pick up 161 sts around neck edge and place on to Ns. Set RC at 000. Using MT and A, K 1 row. Transfer every 3rd st on to adjacent N and push empty Ns to NWP. Using MT-3, K 5 rows. Using MT-4, K 13 rows. Using MT-3, K 4 rows. Push Ns from NWP to WP and place loop from row below adjacent st on to empty Ns. Using MT, K 2 rows. Using WY, K a few rows and release from machine.

TO JOIN LEFT SHOULDER

Work as for right shoulder but read left for right.

TO JOIN SLEEVES TO ARMHOLES

Push 186 Ns to WP. With K side facing, replace 186 sts from top of sleeve on to Ns. Unravel WY. With P side facing, pick up 186 sts along side edge of armhole and place on to same Ns. Using MT and A, K 1 row. Cast off (bind off).

PRESSING

With wrong side facing, pin out pieces to measurements given. Press carefully following instructions on cone band.

MAKING UP

Sew rows above markers on sleeves to cast off (bound off) sts on back and front. Join side and sleeve seams.

Machines with ribber

Join neckband seam. Pin neckband into position. Unravelling WY as required, backstitch through open loops of last row worked in A. Fold in half to wrong side and slipstitch loosely in position.

Machines without ribber

Join neckband seam. Fold in half to right side and pin in position. Unravelling WY as required, backstitch through open loops of last row worked in A.

Lotus Child

A scaled-down version of the adult's Lotus sweater,
making a warm and practical sweater for a boy or girl.

PATTERN RATING
● ● ● ● Recommended for experts only.

MACHINES
This pattern is suitable for standard gauge
punchcard machines.

MATERIALS
Rowan Botany Wool.
270 g (10 oz) in shade 67 (A).
110 g (4 oz) in shade 614 (B).
15 g (1 oz) in shade 45 (C).
25 g (1 oz) in shade 108 (D).
30 g (1 oz) in shade 9 (E).
Rowan Botany Wool is 100% Pure New Wool.

YARN THICKNESS
Medium yarn.

MEASUREMENTS
To fit chest 71-76 cm, 28-30 in.
Actual measurement 84 cm, 33 in.
Length to shoulder 50 cm, 19¾ in.
Sleeve seam 37 cm, 14½ in.

TENSION
32 stitches and 40 rows to 10 cm, 4 in
measured over Fair Isle pattern (tension dial
setting approximately 7).
*For perfect results, your tension must be
matched exactly before starting the
garment.*

ABBREVIATIONS
See page 9.

NOTES
Knit side of knitting is right side of finished
garment.
The card shown on page 83 should be
punched, if required, before starting to knit.
Two colour Fair Isle rows should be knitted
with the first colour given in the back feeder
1(A) to knit the background and the second
colour given in the front feeder 2(B) to knit
the contrast pattern.

FAIR ISLE PATTERN
K four rows A/B, 1 row A only (st st), 2 rows
E/B, 1 row A only (st st), 4 rows A/B, 22 rows
A/C, 1 row A only (st st), 2 rows A/E, 4 rows
A/B, 1 row A only (st st), 2 rows E/B, 1 row A
only (st st), 28 rows A/B, 1 row A only (st st),
2 rows C/B, 1 row A only (st st), 4 rows A/B,
22 rows A/D, 1 row A only (st st), 2 rows A/C,

4 rows A/B, 1 row A only (st st), 2 rows C/B,
1 row A only (st st), 28 rows A/B, 1 row A
only (st st), 2 rows D/B, 1 row A only (st st), 4
rows A/B, 22 rows A/E, 1 row A only (st st), 2
rows A/D, 4 rows A/B, 1 row A only (st st), 2
rows D/B, 1 row A only (st st) and 4 rows A/B.

BACK
Machines with ribber
With ribber in position and carriage at right,
set machine for 1×1 rib. Push 68 Ns at left
and right of centre 0 to WP. 136 Ns. Push
corresponding Ns on ribber to WP. Arrange
Ns for 1×1 rib. Using A, cast on and K 3
tubular rows. Carriage is at right. Set
carriage for 1×1 rib knitting. Set RC at 000.
Using MT-6/MT-6, K 14 rows. Transfer sts for
st st.
Machines without ribber
Push 67 Ns at left and right of centre 0 to
WP. 134 Ns. Push every 3rd N back to NWP.
Using MT and WY, cast on and K a few rows
ending with carriage at left. Set RC at 000.
Using MT-4 and A, K 25 rows. Push Ns from
NWP to WP and make a hem by placing
loops of first row worked in A evenly along
the row. Unravel WY, when work is
completed. Inc 1 st at each end. 136 sts.
All machines
Insert punchcard and lock on first row. Set

carriage for patt. Set RC at 000. Using MT,
K 1 row. Release card and cont in Fair Isle
patt. K 109 rows. RC shows 110 and work
measures 30 cm, 11¾ in.
Shape armholes Cast off (bind off) 18 sts at
beg of next 2 rows. 100 sts *.
K 72 rows.
Shape neck Note patt row on card. Using a
length of A, cast off (bind off) centre 58 sts.
Using nylon cord, K 21 sts at left by hand
taking Ns down to NWP. Cont on rem sts for
first side.
K 1 row. Dec 1 st at beg of next and foll alt
row. 19 sts. Cont in st st and A, K 2 rows.
Using WY, K a few rows and release from
machine.
With carriage at right, unravel nylon cord
over rem Ns bringing Ns back to WP. Lock
card on number previously noted. Take
carriage to left without knitting. Release
card and cont in Fair Isle patt. Finish to
correspond with first side reversing shapings.

FRONT
Work as for back to *.
K 61 rows.
Shape neck Note patt row on card. Using a
length of A, cast off (bind off) centre 46 sts.
Using nylon cord, K 27 sts at right by hand
taking Ns down to NWP. Cont on rem sts for
first side.
Dec 1 st at neck edge of next and every foll
alt row until 19 sts rem. Cont in st st and A,
K 2 rows. Using WY, K a few rows and
release from machine.
With carriage at left, unravel nylon cord over
rem Ns bringing Ns back to WP. Lock card
on number previously noted. Take carriage
to right without knitting. Release card and
cont in Fair Isle patt. Finish to correspond
with first side reversing shapings.

SLEEVES
Machines with ribber
With ribber in position and carriage at right,
set machine for 1×1 rib. Push 31 Ns at left
and right of centre 0 to WP. 62 Ns. Push
corresponding Ns on ribber to WP. Arrange
Ns for 1×1 rib. Using A, cast on and K 3
tubular rows. Carriage is at right. Set
carriage for 1×1 rib knitting. Set RC at 000.
Using MT-6/MT-6, K 26 rows. Transfer sts
for st st.
Machines without ribber
Push 31 Ns at left and right of centre 0 to

81

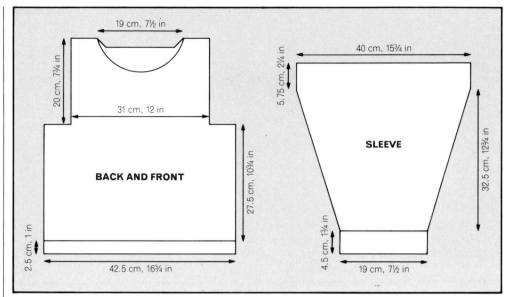

WP. 62 Ns. Push every 3rd N back to NWP. Using MT and WY, cast on and K a few rows ending with carriage at left. Set RC at 000. Using MT-4 and A, K 47 rows. Push Ns from NWP to WP and make a hem by placing loops of first row worked in A evenly along the row. Unravel WY when work is completed.

All machines

Insert punchcard and lock on 38th row. Set carriage for patt. Set RC at 000. Using MT, K 1 row. Release card and cont in Fair Isle patt (starting with 38th row). Shape sides by inc 1 st at each end of next and every foll 4th row until there are 128 sts. RC shows 130 and work measures 37 cm, 14½ in. Place marker at each end. K 21 rows. Cont in st st and A, K 2 rows. Using WY, K a few rows and release from machine.

COLLAR
Machines with ribber

With ribber in position and carriage at right, set machine for full needle rib/double rib. Push 140 Ns on both beds to WP for full needle rib/double rib. Using A, cast on and K 3 tubular rows. Carriage is at right. Set carriage for full needle rib/double rib knitting. Set RC at 000. Using MT-4/MT-4, K 35 rows. Transfer sts to main bed. Cast off (bind off).

Machines without ribber

Push 155 Ns to WP. Push every 3rd N back to NWP. Using MT and WY, cast on and K a few rows ending with carriage at left. Set RC at 000. Using MT-4 and A, K 17 rows. Using MT-3, K 37 rows. Using MT-4, K 17 rows. Push Ns from NWP to WP and make a hem by placing loops of first row worked in A evenly along the row. Unravel WY when work is completed. Using MT, K 2 rows. Using WY, K a few rows and release from machine.

TO JOIN RIGHT SHOULDER

Push 19 Ns to WP. With K side of right back shoulder facing, replace sts on to Ns. Unravel WY. With P side of right front

shoulder facing, replace sts on to same Ns. Unravel WY. Using MT and A, K 1 row. Cast off (bind off).

TO JOIN LEFT SHOULDER

Work as for right shoulder but read left for right.

TO JOIN SLEEVES TO ARMHOLES

Push 128 Ns to WP, With K side facing, replace 128 sts from top of sleeve on to Ns. Unravel WY. With P side facing, pick up 128 sts along side edge of armhole and place on to same Ns. Using MT and A, K 1 row. Cast off (bind off).

PRESSING

With wrong side facing, pin out pieces to measurements given. Press carefully following instructions on cone band.

MAKING UP

Sew rows above markers on sleeves to cast off (bound off) sts on back and front. Join side, sleeve and collar seam.
Machines with ribber
Sew cast off (bound off) edge of collar into position with seam at centre back.
Machines without ribber
Pin collar into position with seam at centre back. Unravelling WY as required, backstitch through open loops of last row worked in A.
All machines
Fold collar in half to right side.

Diamond Dress

A warm winter dress worn belted or straight. Length
can be altered by omitting a sequence of the diamond repeat.

84 PATTERN RATING
●●●● Recommended for experts only.

MACHINES
This pattern is suitable for standard gauge
punchcard machines.

MATERIALS
Rowan Botany Wool.
310 g (11 oz) in shade 84 (A).
325 g (12 oz) in shade 635 (B).
115 g (4 oz) in shade 62 (C).
25 g (1 oz) in shade 9 (D).
15 g (½ oz) in shade 108 (E).
Rowan Botany Wool is 100% Pure New Wool.

YARN THICKNESS
Medium yarn.

MEASUREMENTS
To fit chest 87-97 cm, 34-38 in.
Actual measurement 125 cm, 49¼ in.
Length to shoulder 96.5 cm, 38 in.
Sleeve seam 48.25 cm, 19 in.

TENSION
31 stitches and 39 rows to 10 cm, 4 in
measured over Fair Isle pattern (tension dial
setting approximately 7).
*For perfect results, your tension must be
matched exactly before starting the
garment.*

ABBREVIATIONS
See page 9.

NOTES
Knit side of knitting is right side of finished
garment.
The cards shown on page 85 should be
punched, if required, before starting to knit.
Two colour Fair Isle rows should be knitted
with the first colour given in the back feeder
1(A) to knit the background and the second
colour given in the front feeder 2(B) to knit
the contrast pattern.

FAIR ISLE PATTERN
Back and front
K 13 rows A/C, 2 rows A only (st st), 5 rows
A/D, 2 rows A only (st st), 13 rows A/C, 2
rows A only (st st), 5 rows A/E, 2 rows A only
(st st), * 13 rows A/B, 2 rows A only (st st), 5
rows A/C, 2 rows A only (st st); rep from * 6
times more, 13 rows A/B, 2 rows A only (st

st), 5 rows A/D, 2 rows A only (st st), 7 rows
A/C, 6 rows B/C, 2 rows B only (st st), 5
rows B/D, 1 row B only (st st). Remove card.
Insert punchcard 2 and lock on first row. K 1
row B only (st st). Release card. K 16 rows
B/A, 2 rows B only (st st), 5 rows B/D, 2
rows B only (st st), 16 rows B/A, 2 rows B
only (st st), 5 rows B/E, 2 rows B only (st st),
16 rows B/C, 2 rows B only (st st), 5 rows

*The style of the Lotus Child sweater is
echoed in the Diamond Dress, which has
been knitted in soft muted colours.*

B/E, 2 rows B only (st st), 16 rows B/C, 2
rows B only (st st), 5 rows B/D, 2 rows B
only (st st), 16 rows B/A, 2 rows B only (st
st), 5 rows B/D and 2 rows B only (st st).

Sleeves K 13 rows A/C, 2 rows A only (st st), 5 rows A/D, 2 rows A only (st st), 13 rows A/C, 2 rows A only (st st), 5 rows A/E, 2 rows A only (st st), 13 rows A/B, 2 rows A only (st st), 5 rows A/C, 2 rows A only (st st), 13 rows A/B, 2 rows A only (st st), 5 rows A/C, 2 rows A only (st st), 13 rows A/B, 2 rows A only (st st), 5 rows A/D, 2 rows A only (st st), 7 rows A/C, 6 rows B/C, 2 rows B only (st st), 5 rows B/D, 1 row B only (st st). Remove card. Insert punchcard 2 and lock on first row. K 1 row B only (st st). Release card. K 16 rows B/A, 2 rows B only (st st), 5 rows B/D, 2 rows B only (st st), 16 rows B/A, 2 rows B only (st st), 5 rows B/E, 2 rows B only (st st), 16 rows B/C and 2 rows B only (st st).

BACK
Machines with ribber
With ribber in position and carriage at right, set machine for 1×1 rib. Push 90 Ns at left and right of centre 0 to WP. 180 Ns.
* Push corresponding Ns on ribber to WP. Arrange Ns for 1×1 rib. Using B, cast on and K 3 tubular rows. Carriage is at right. Set carriage for 1×1 rib knitting. Set RC at 000. Using MT-6/MT-6, K 14 rows. Transfer sts for st st *.

Machines without ribber
Push 90 Ns at left and 89 Ns at right of centre 0 to WP. 179 Ns.
* Push every 3rd N back to NWP. Using MT and WY, cast on and K a few rows ending with carriage at left. Set RC at 000. Using MT-4 and B, K 25 rows. Push Ns from NWP to WP and make a hem by placing loops of first row worked in B evenly along the row. Unravel WY when work is completed *.
Inc 1 st at right edge. 180 sts.

All machines
Insert punchcard 1 and lock on first row. Set carriage for patt. Set RC at 000. Using MT and A, K 1 row. Release card and cont in Fair Isle patt. K 18 rows. Shape sides by inc 1 st at each end of next and every foll 20th row until there are 196 sts. K 99 rows. RC shows 259 and work measures 68.5 cm, 27 in.
Shape armholes Cast off (bind off) 18 sts at beg of next 2 rows. 160 sts **.
K 100 rows.
Shape neck Note patt row on card. Using a length of B, cast off (bind off) centre 68 sts. Using nylon cord, K 46 sts at right by hand taking Ns down to NWP. Cont on rem sts for first side.
K 1 row. Dec 1 st at beg of next and foll alt row. 44 sts. K 3 rows.
Using WY, K a few rows in st st and release from machine.
With carriage at left, unravel nylon cord over rem Ns bringing Ns back to WP. Lock card on number previously noted. Take carriage to right without knitting. Release card and cont in Fair Isle patt.
Finish to correspond with first side reversing shapings.

FRONT
Work as for back to **. K 82 rows.

Shape neck Note patt row on card. Using a length of B, cast off (bind off) centre 54 sts. Using nylon cord, K 53 sts at right by hand taking Ns down to NWP. Cont on rem sts for first side.
K 1 row. Dec 1 st (2 sts in) at beg of next and every foll alt row until 44 sts rem. K 7 rows.
Using WY, K a few rows in st st and release from machine.
With carriage at left, unravel nylon cord over rem Ns bringing Ns back to WP. Lock card on number previously noted. Take carriage to right without knitting. Release card and cont in Fair Isle patt. Finish to correspond with first side reversing shapings.

SLEEVES
Machines with ribber
With ribber in position and carriage at right, set machine for 1×1 rib. Push 37 Ns at left and right of centre 0 to WP. 74 Ns. Work as for back from * to *.
Machines without ribber
Push 37 Ns at left and right of centre 0 to WP. 74 Ns. Work as for back from * to *.
All machines
Insert punchcard 1 and lock on first row. Set carriage for patt. Set RC at 000. Using MT and A, K 1 row. Release card and cont in Fair Isle patt. K 1 row. Shape sides by inc 1 st at each end of next and every foll 3rd row until there are 174 sts. K 29 rows.
RC shows 179 and work measures 48.25 cm, 19 in.
Place marker at each end. K 22 rows. Using WY, K a few rows in st st and release from machine.

COLLAR
Machines with ribber
With ribber in position and carriage at right, set carriage for full needle rib/double rib. Push 140 Ns on both beds to WP for full needle rib/double rib. Using B, cast on and K 3 tubular rows. Carriage is at right. Set carriage for full needle rib/double rib knitting. Set RC at 000. Using MT-4/MT-4, K 50 rows. Transfer sts to main bed. Cast off (bind off).

Machines without ribber
Push 179 Ns to WP. Push every 3rd N back to NWP. Using MT and WY, cast on and K a few rows ending with carriage at left. Set RC at 000. Using MT-4 and B, K 24 rows. Using MT-3, K 51 rows. Using MT-4, K 24 rows. Push Ns from NWP to WP and make a hem by placing loops of first row worked in B evenly along the row. Unravel WY when work is completed. Using MT, K 2 rows. Using WY, K a few rows and release from machine.

TO JOIN RIGHT SHOULDER
Push 44 Ns to WP. With K side of right back shoulder facing, replace sts on to Ns. Unravel WY. With P side of right front shoulder facing, replace sts on to same Ns. Unravel WY. Using MT and B, K 1 row. Cast off (bind off).

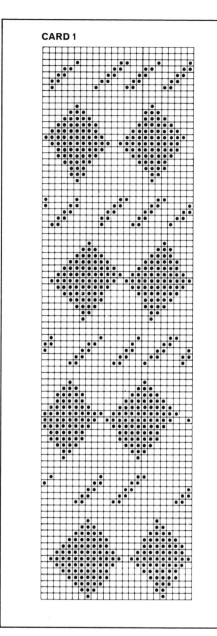

CARD 1

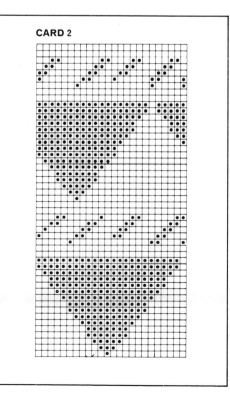

CARD 2

85

TO JOIN LEFT SHOULDER

Work as for right shoulder but read left for right.

TO JOIN SLEEVES TO ARMHOLES

Push 174 Ns to WP. With K side facing, replace 174 sts from top of sleeve on to Ns. Unravel WY. With P side facing, pick up 174 sts along side edge of armhole and place on to same Ns. Using MT and B, K 1 row. Cast off (bind off).

PRESSING

With wrong side facing, pin out pieces to measurements given. Press carefully following instructions on cone band.

MAKING UP

Sew rows above markers on sleeves to cast off (bound off) sts on back and front. Join side, sleeve and collar seams.

Machines with ribber

Sew cast off (bound off) edge of collar into position with seam at centre back.

Machines without ribber

Pin collar into position with seam at centre back. Unravelling WY as required, backstitch through open loops of last row worked in B.

All machines

Fold collar in half to right side.

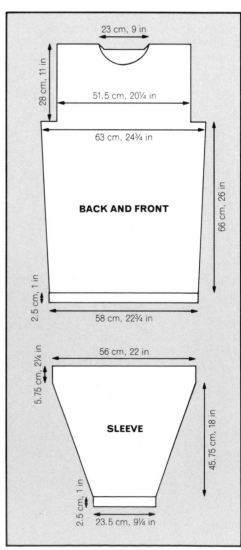

Rough Diamond

A colourful, relaxed woollen
cardigan with practical pockets – ideal
for winter, or, alternatively, in cotton with paler colours for spring.

PATTERN RATING
● ● ● ● Recommended for experts only.

MACHINES
This pattern is suitable for standard gauge punchcard machines.

MATERIALS
Rowan Botany Wool.
260 g (9½ oz) in shade 60 (A).
320 g (11½ oz) in shade 62 (B).
100 g (4 oz) in shade 45 (C).
30 g (1 oz) in shade 9 (D).
20 g (1 oz) in shade 108 (E).
6 buttons.
Rowan Botany Wool is 100% Pure New Wool.

YARN THICKNESS
Medium yarn.

MEASUREMENTS
To fit chest 87-97 cm, 34-38 in.
Actual measurement 125 cm, 49¼ in.
Length to shoulder 73.5 cm, 29 in.
Sleeve seam 48.25 cm, 19 in.

TENSION
31 stitches and 39 rows to 10 cm, 4 in
measured over Fair Isle pattern (tension dial
setting appropximately 7).
*For perfect results, your tension must be
matched exactly before starting the
garment.*

ABBREVIATIONS
See page 9.

NOTES
Knit side of knitting is right side of finished
garment.
The cards shown on page 90 should be
punched, if required, before starting to knit.
Two colour Fair Isle rows should be knitted
with the first colour given in the back feeder
1(A) to knit the background and the second
colour given in the front feeder 2(B) to knit
the contrast pattern.

FAIR ISLE PATTERN
Back, fronts and pockets
K 13 rows A/C, 2 rows A only (st st), 5 rows
A/D, 2 rows A only (st st), 13 rows A/C, 2
rows A only (st st), 5 rows A/E, 2 rows A only
(st st), * 13 rows A/B, 2 rows A only (st st), 5
rows A/C, 2 rows A only (st st); rep from * 3

times more, 13 rows A/B, 2 rows A only (st st), 5 rows A/D, 2 rows A only (st st), 7 rows A/C, 6 rows B/C, 2 rows B only (st st), 2 rows B/D, 1 row B only (st st). Remove card. Insert punchcard 2 and lock on first row. K 1 row B only (st st). Release card. K 16 rows B/A, 2 rows B only (st st), 5 rows B/D, 2 rows B only (st st), 16 rows B/A, 2 rows B only (st st), 16 rows B/C, 2 rows B only (st st), 5 rows B/E, 2 rows B only (st st), 5 rows B/E, 2 rows B only (st st), 16 rows B/C, 2 rows B only (st st), 5 rows B/E and 2 rows B only (st st).

Sleeves K 13 rows A/C, 2 rows A only (st st), 5 rows A/D, 2 rows A only (st st), 13 rows A/C, 2 rows A only (st st), 5 rows A/E, 2 rows A only (st st), 13 rows A/B, 2 rows A only (st st), 5 rows A/C, 2 rows A only (st st), 13 rows A/B, 2 rows A only (st st), 5 rows A/C, 2 rows A only (st st), 13 rows A/B, 2 rows A only (st st), 5 rows A/D, 2 rows A only (st st), 7 rows A/C, 6 rows B/C, 2 rows B only (st st), 5 rows B/D, 1 row B only (st st). Remove card. Insert punchcard 2 and lock on first row. K 1 row B only (st st). Release card. K 16 rows B/A, 2 rows B only (st st), 5 rows B/D, 2 rows B only (st st), 16 rows B/A, 2 rows B only (st st), 5 rows B/E, 2 rows B only (st st), 16 rows B/C and 2 rows B only (st st).

BACK

Machines with ribber

With ribber in position and carriage at right, set machine for 1×1 rib. Push 90 Ns at left and right of centre 0 to WP. 180 Ns.

* Push corresponding Ns on ribber to WP. Arrange Ns for 1×1 rib. Using B, cast on and K 3 tubular rows. Carriage is at right. Set carriage for 1×1 rib knitting. Set RC at 000. Using MT-6/MT-6, K 14 rows. Transfer sts for st st *.

Machines without ribber

Push 90 Ns at left and 89 Ns at right of centre 0 to WP. 179 Ns.

* Push every 3rd N back to NWP. Using MT and WY, cast on and K a few rows ending with carriage at left. Set RC at 000. Using MT-4 and B, K 25 rows. Push Ns from NWP to WP and make a hem by placing loops of first row worked in B evenly along the row. Unravel WY when work is completed *.

Inc 1 st at right edge. 180 sts.

All machines

Insert punchcard 1 and lock on first row. Set carriage for patt. Set RC at 000. Using MT and A, K 1 row. Release card and cont in Fair Isle patt. K 18 rows. Shape sides by inc 1 st at each end of next and every foll 20th row until there are 196 sts. K 2 rows. RC shows 162 and work measures 44 cm, 17¼ in.

Shape armholes Cast off (bind off) 18 sts at beg of next 2 rows. 160 sts. K 106 rows.

Shape neck Note patt row on card. Using a length of B, cast off (bind off) centre 58 sts. Using nylon cord, K 51 sts at left by hand taking Ns down to NWP. Cont on rem sts for first side.

K 1 row. Dec 1 st at beg of next and foll alt row. 49 sts. K 3 rows. Using WY, K a few rows in st st and release from machine.

With carriage at right, unravel nylon cord over rem Ns bringing Ns back to WP. Lock card on number previously noted. Take carriage to left without knitting. Release card and cont in Fair Isle patt. Finish to correspond with first side reversing shapings.

RIGHT FRONT

Machines with ribber

With ribber in position and carriage at right, set machine for 1×1 rib. Push 43 Ns at left and right of centre 0 to WP. 86 Ns. Work as for back from * to *.

Machines without ribber

Push 43 Ns at left and right of centre 0 to WP. 86 Ns. Work as for back from * to *.

All machines

Insert punchcard 1 and lock on first row. Set carriage for patt. Set RC at 000. Using MT and A, K 1 row. Release card and cont in Fair Isle patt. K 18 rows. Shape side by inc 1 st at right edge (left edge on left front) of next and every foll 20th row until there are 94 sts. K 2 rows. RC shows 162 and work measures 44 cm, 17¼ in. K 1 row extra for left front.

Shape armhole Cast off (bind off) 18 sts at beg of next row. 76 sts. K 82 rows.

Shape neck Cast off (bind off) 15 sts at beg of next row. Dec 1 st (2 sts in) at neck edge on every row until 49 sts rem. K 19 rows (18 rows only on left front). Using WY, K a few rows in st st and release from machine.

LEFT FRONT

Work as for right front but reverse shapings by noting alteration in number of rows worked.

SLEEVES

Machines with ribber

With ribber in position and carriage at right, set machine for 1×1 rib. Push 37 Ns at left and right of centre 0 to WP. 74 Ns. Work as for back from * to *.

Machines without ribber

Push 37 Ns at left and right of centre 0 to WP. 74 Ns. Work as for back from * to *.

All machines

Insert punchcard 1 and lock on first row. Set carriage for patt. Set RC at 000. Using MT and A, K 1 row. Release card and cont in Fair Isle patt. K 1 row. Shape sides by inc 1 st at each end of next and every foll 3rd row until there are 184 sts. K 14 rows. RC shows 179 and work measures 48.25 cm, 19 in. Place marker at each end. K 22 rows. Using WY, K a few rows in st st and release from machine.

POCKETS

Insert punchcard 1 and lock on first row. Push 22 Ns at left and right of centre 0 to WP. 44 Ns. Using MT and WY, cast on and K a few rows ending with carriage at right. Set RC at 000. Release card and cont in Fair Isle patt. K 44 rows. Using WY, K a few rows in st st and release from machine.

POCKET TOPS

Machines with ribber

With ribber in position and carriage at right, set machine for 1×1 rib. Push 44 Ns to WP. Work as for back from * to *.

Machines without ribber

Push 44 Ns to WP. Work as for back from * to *.

All machines

With P side of pocket facing, replace sts from last row on to Ns. Unravel WY. Using MT and B, K 1 row. Cast off (bind off).

TO JOIN RIGHT SHOULDER

Push 49 Ns to WP. With K side of right back shoulder facing, replace sts on to Ns. Unravel WY. With P side of right front shoulder facing, replace sts on to same Ns. Unravel WY. Using MT and B, K 1 row. Cast off (bind off).

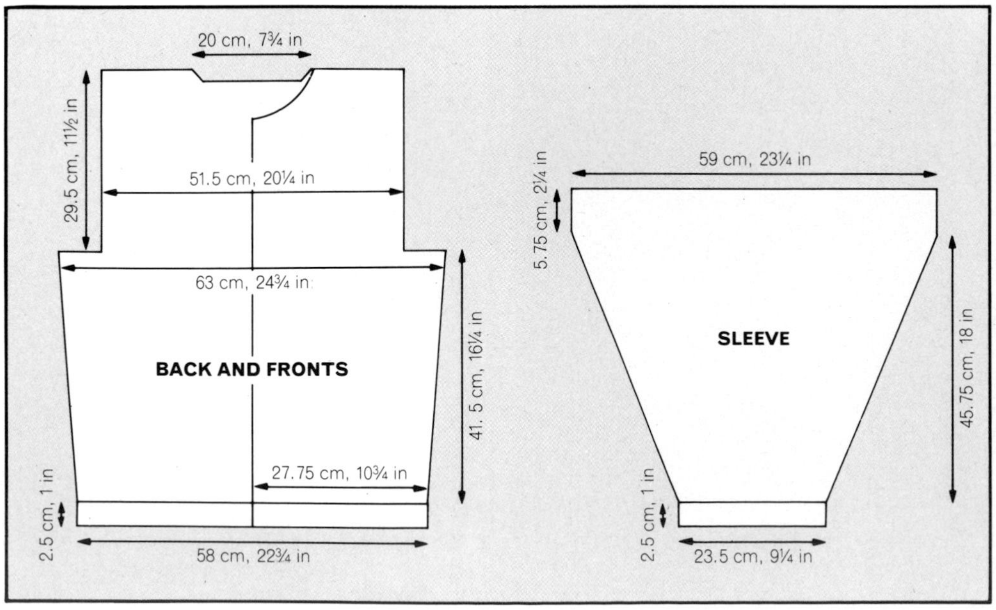
20 cm, 7¾ in
29.5 cm, 11½ in
51.5 cm, 20¼ in
63 cm, 24¾ in
BACK AND FRONTS
41. 5 cm, 16¼ in
27.75 cm, 10¾ in
2.5 cm, 1 in
58 cm, 22¾ in
5.75 cm, 2¼ in
59 cm, 23¼ in
SLEEVE
45.75 cm, 18 in
2.5 cm, 1 in
23.5 cm, 9¼ in

Lotus sweater and Rough Diamond cardigan are ideal to wear for the outdoor life.

TO JOIN LEFT SHOULDER

Work as for right shoulder but read left for right.

NECKBAND
Machines with ribber

With ribber in position and carriage at right, set machine for 1×1 rib. Using B, cast on 165 sts in 1×1 rib. K 3 tubular rows. Carriage is at right. Set carriage for 1×1 rib knitting. Set RC at 000. Using MT-6/MT-6, K 28 rows. Transfer sts for st st. Using WY, K a few rows and release from machine.

Machines without ribber

Push 167 Ns to WP. With K side facing, pick up 167 sts around neck edge and place on to Ns. Set RC at 000. Using MT and B, K 1 row. Transfer every 3rd st on to adjacent N and push empty Ns to NWP. Using MT-3, K 5 rows. Using MT-4, K 13 rows. Using MT-3, K 4 rows. Push Ns from NWP to WP and place loop from row below adjacent st on to empty Ns. Using MT, K 2 rows. Using WY, K a few rows and release from machine. Fold in half to right side and pin in position. Unravelling WY as required, backstitch through open loops of last row worked in B.

BUTTONHOLE BAND
Machines with ribber

With ribber in position and carriage at right, set machine for 1×1 rib. Using B, cast on 15 sts in 1×1 rib. K 3 tubular rows. Carriage is at right. Set carriage for 1×1 rib knitting. Set RC at 000.

Knitmaster machines

Push main bed left side lever back and right side lever forward. Set cam lever to slip, leave ribber to knit normally.

Brother machines

Press right part button.

All machines

Using MT-7/MT-7, K 7 rows.
* Make a buttonhole by transferring centre st on to adjacent N. Leave empty N in WP. K 59 rows. Rep from * 4 times more. Make another buttonhole over same Ns as before. K 8 rows. RC shows 310. Transfer sts to main bed. Cast off (bind off).

Machines without ribber

Push 190 Ns to WP. With K side facing, pick up 190 sts along right front edge and place on to Ns. Set RC at 000. Using MT-1 and B, K 5 rows. Make 6 evenly spaced buttonholes. K 11 rows. Make buttonholes over same Ns as before, K 5 rows. Using WY, K a few rows and release from machine.

BUTTON BAND
Machines with ribber

Work as for buttonhole band omitting buttonholes.

Machines without ribber

Work as for buttonhole band omitting buttonholes and reading left for right.

TO JOIN SLEEVES TO ARMHOLES

Push 184 Ns to WP. With K side facing,

CARD 1

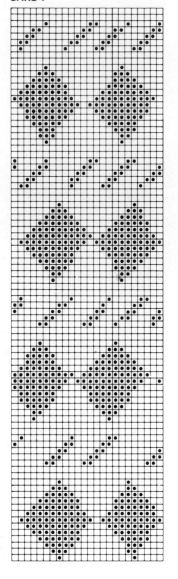

CARD 2

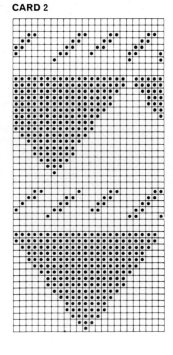

replace 184 sts from top of sleeve on to Ns. Unravel WY. With P side facing, pick up 184 sts along side edge of armhole and place on to same Ns. Using MT and B, K 1 row. Cast off (bind off).

PRESSING

With wrong side facing, pin out pieces to measurements given. Press carefully following instructions on cone band.

MAKING UP

Sew rows above markers on sleeves to cast off (bound off) sts on back and front. Join side and sleeve seams. Graft lower edge of pockets into position. Sew sides into position.

Machines with ribber

Pin neckband into position. Unravelling WY as required, back stitch through open loops of last row worked in B. Fold in half to wrong side and slipstitch loosely in position. Sew front bands into position. Sew on buttons.

Machines without ribber

Fold front bands in half to right side and pin in position. Unravelling WY as required, backstitch through open loops of last row worked in B. Neaten ends of bands. Finish buttonholes. Sew on buttons.

90

Summer Classics

This section consists of plain sweaters and cabled sweaters. It is refreshing for the experienced knitter and obviously ideal for a beginner to keep things simple. It's also a pleasant change to wear a plain sweater.

The Black and White sweater/dress uses the simple technique of using two contrasting colours. The bold stripes are enhanced by the use of a light, slightly textured yarn. Yarns with a silk content (or, as a less expensive alternative, acrylic) allow the shape to drape so that the pieces can be larger without becoming stiff or heavy. The boat neck has a ribbed collar which is open at each shoulder. As an alternative, you could centre the collar at the front and back. In this garment the stripe width is halved at the top of the sleeves fitting into the deep armhole inset. Try playing around with different stripe rhythms; if you want to create a more subtle effect you could use less contrasting colours.

Cabled Silk top and skirt and the Tea Rose Cardigan and Camisole are knitted in pure silk but, again, given the same stitch specification, they could be knitted in cotton or a mixture yarn to produce a more casual look. The top is cabled along the top, forming a yoke effect, and the trimming is the same width as the cables. It can be worn independently or, as illustrated, with the skirt, which is simple to make with an elasticized waist band and easy to adjust in length by omitting or adding rows to the pattern.

Tea Rose Cardigan has three rows of cables running down the centre back as well as on both sides of the front. This of course can be omitted, but it forms a nice detail that gives some interest to the back as well. The two small pockets and the fine ribs make it intentionally traditional, an effect enhanced by the choice of buttons, which in this case are antique glass. The camisole top worn underneath is perfect for summer and makes a practical twinset when worn with the cardigan. The cable detail on the yoke echoes the cabling on the cardigan, although both garments can be worn on their own.

The Metropolitan sweater/dress is made in a mixture of silk and wool, producing an interesting surface effect. The collar is a single-bed piece of knitting folded over – remember to sew the crossover neatly, as this becomes a focus of attention. The sweater looks best if different shades of the same colour are used, and works well in restrained neutral colours like cream and beige or brown and black.

For all the sweaters in this section, take extra care when knitting and finishing to make sure there are no snags in the knitting or tucks through bad stitching. Because there is no distraction for the eye, as with Fair Isle patterns, flaws become much more noticeable.

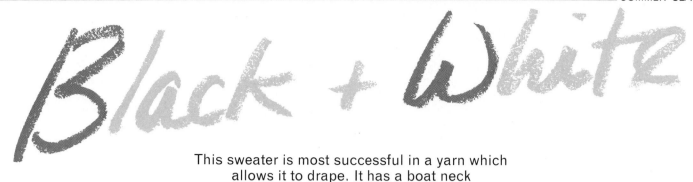

Black + White

This sweater is most successful in a yarn which
allows it to drape. It has a boat neck
with collar and narrower stripes at the sleeve inset.

PATTERN RATING
● Easy to knit.

MACHINES
This pattern is suitable for standard gauge
machines.

MATERIALS
Silk and cotton.
300 g (11 oz) in black (MC).
275 g (10 oz) in ecru (C).

YARN THICKNESS
Medium-textured yarn.

MEASUREMENTS
To fit chest 87-97 cm, 34-38 in.
Actual measurement 167 cm, 65¾ in.
Length to shoulder 84 cm, 33 in.
Sleeve seam 32.5 cm, 12¾ in.

TENSION
23 stitches and 35 rows to 10 cm, 4 in
measured over stocking stitch (tension dial
setting approximately 10).
*For perfect results, your tension must be
matched exactly before starting the
garment.*

ABBREVIATIONS
See page 9.

NOTES
Knit side of knitting is right side of finished
garment.

STRIPE PATTERN
K 8 rows MC.
* K 16 rows C and 16 rows MC. Repeat
from *.

BACK AND FRONT (Alike)
Machines with ribber
With ribber in position and carriage at right,
set machine for 1×1 rib. Push 69 Ns at left
and right of centre 0 to WP. 138 Ns.
* Push corresponding Ns on ribber to WP.
Arrange Ns for 1×1 rib. Using MC, cast on
and K 3 tubular rows. Carriage is at right.
Set carriage for 1×1 rib knitting. Set RC at
000. Using MT-4/MT-4, K 8 rows. Transfer
sts for st st *.
Machines without ribber
Push 69 Ns at left and 68 Ns at right of
centre 0 to WP. 137 Ns.

* Push every 3rd N back to NWP. Using MT
and WY, cast on and K a few rows ending
with carriage at left. Set RC at 000. Using
MT-2 and MC, K 19 rows. Push Ns from
NWP to WP and make a hem by placing
loops of first row worked in MC evenly along
the row. Unravel WY when work is
completed *.
Inc 1 st at right edge. 138 sts.
All machines
Set RC at 000. Using MT, cont in stripe patt.
K 5 rows. Shape sides by inc 1 st at each
end of next and every foll 6th row until there
are 194 sts. K 16 rows. RC shows 184 and
work measures 54.5 cm, 21½ in.
Shape armholes Cast off (bind off) 40 sts
at beg of next 2 rows. 114 sts. K 96 rows.
Shape neck Using a length of MC, cast off
(bind off) centre 62 sts. Push 26 Ns at left to
HP and cont on rem sts for first side.
K 1 row. Dec 1 st at beg of next and foll alt
row. 24 sts. K 2 rows. Using WY, K a few
rows and release from machine. With
carriage at left, push rem Ns from HP to
UWP and finish to correspond with first
side, reversing shapings.

SLEEVES
Machines with ribber
With ribber in position and carriage at right,
set machine for 1×1 rib. Push 23 Ns at left
and right of centre 0 to WP. 46 Ns. Work as
for back and front from * to *.
Machines without ribber
Push 22 Ns at left and right of centre 0 to
WP. 44 Ns. Work as for back and front from
* to *. Inc 1 st at each end. 46 sts.
All machines
Set RC at 000. Using MT, cont in stripe patt.
Shape sides by inc 1 st at each end of next
and every foll alt row until there are 136 sts.
K 15 rows. Cont in stripes of 8 rows C and 8
rows MC, K 3 rows. RC shows 107 and work
measures 32.5 cm, 12¾ in. Place marker at
each end. K 61 rows. Using WY, K a few
rows and release from machine.

NECKBAND (Two pieces)
Machines with ribber
With ribber in position and carriage at right,
set machine for 1×1 rib. Using MC, cast on
80 sts in 1×1 rib. K 3 tubular rows. Carriage
is at right. Set carriage for 1×1 rib knitting.
Set RC at 000. Using MT-4/MT-4, K 15 rows.
Using MT-3/MT-3, K 15 rows. Transfer sts for

st st. Using WY, K a few rows and release
from machine.
Machines without ribber
Push 80 Ns to WP. With K side facing, pick
up 80 sts around neck edge and place on to
Ns. Set RC at 000. Using MT and MC, K 1
row. Transfer every 3rd st on to adjacent N
and push empty Ns to NWP. Using MT-1, K
14 rows. Using MT-2, K 31 rows. Using
MT-1, K 13 rows. Push Ns from NWP to WP
and place loop from row below adjacent st
on to empty Ns. Using MT, K 2 rows. Using
WY, K a few rows and release from
machine.

TO JOIN RIGHT SHOULDER
Push 24 Ns to WP. With K side of right back
shoulder facing, replace sts on to Ns.
Unravel WY. With P side of right front
shoulder facing, replace sts on to same Ns.
Unravel WY. Using MT and MC, K 1 row.
Cast off (bind off).

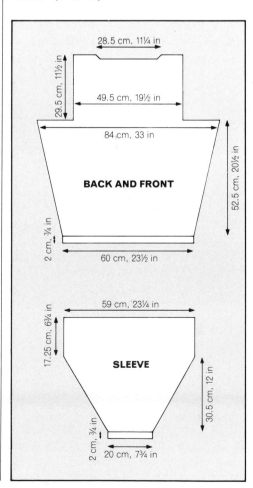

TO JOIN LEFT SHOULDER
Work as for right shoulder, reading left for
right.

TO JOIN SLEEVES TO ARMHOLES
Push 136 Ns to WP. With K side facing,
replace 136 sts from top of sleeve on to Ns.
Unravel WY. With P side facing, pick up 136
sts along side edge of armhole and place on
to same Ns. Using MT and MC, K 1 row.
Cast off (bind off).

PRESSING
With wrong side facing, pin out to
measurements given.
Press carefully following instructions on
cone band.

MAKING UP
Sew rows above markers on sleeves to cast
off (bound off) sts on back and front. Join
sleeve and side seams, leaving 14 cm, 5½ in
open from lower edge.

Machines with ribber
Pin neckbands into position. Unravelling WY
as required backstitch through open loops of
last row worked in MC.
Machines without ribber
Fold neckband in half to outside and pin in
position.
Unravelling WY as required, backstitch
through the open loops of the last row
worked in MC.
Neaten open ends.

Tea Rose

This simple, cabled camisole top is perfect for summer, and makes a practical twin-set when worn with the Tea Rose Cardigan.

PATTERN RATING
● ● Fairly easy, for knitters with some experience.

MACHINES
This pattern is suitable for standard gauge machines.

MATERIALS
Rowan Mulberry Silk.
200 [225, 250] g (7 [8, 9] oz) in shade 870 (MY).

YARN THICKNESS
Medium heavy yarn.

MEASUREMENTS
To fit chest 76-82 [87-92, 97-102] cm, 30-32 [34-36, 38-40] in.
Actual size 85 [95, 105] cm, 33½ [37½, 41½] in.
Length to shoulder 40 [41, 42] cm, 15¾ [16¼, 16½] in.
Instructions are written for the smallest size, larger sizes follow in square brackets. If only one figure is given, it applies to all sizes.

TENSION
29 stitches and 42 rows to 10 cm, 4 in measured over stocking stitch (tension dial setting approximately 7).
For perfect results, your tension must be matched exactly before starting the garment.

ABBREVIATIONS
See page 9.

NOTES
Knit side of knitting is right side of finished garment.

CABLE PATTERN
Cross sts 1 and 2 in front of sts 3 and 4, K 4 rows. Cross sts 1 and 2 in front of sts 3 and 4, K 4 rows.
Cross sts 1 and 2 in front of sts 3 and 4 and sts 5 and 6 in front of sts 7 and 8, K 4 rows.
Cross sts 1 and 2 in front of sts 3 and 4 and sts 5 and 6 in front of sts 7 and 8, K 4 rows.
Cross sts 1 and 2 in front of sts 3 and 4, sts 5 and 6 in front of sts 7 and 8 and sts 9 and 10 in front of sts 11 and 12, K 4 rows.
Cross sts 1 and 2 in front of sts 3 and 4, sts 5 and 6 in front of sts 7 and 8 and sts 9 and 10 in front of sts 11 and 12, K 4 rows.

Cross sts 1 and 2 in front of sts 3 and 4, sts 5 and 6 in front of sts 7 and 8, sts 9 and 10 in front of sts 11 and 12 and sts 13 and 14 in front of sts 15 and 16, K 4 rows.

Cross sts 1 and 2 in front of sts 3 and 4, sts 5 and 6 in front of sts 7 and 8, sts 9 and 10 in front of sts 11 and 12 and sts 13 and 14 in front of sts 15 and 16, K 4 rows.

* Cross sts 1 and 2 in front of sts 3 and 4, sts 5 and 6 in front of sts 7 and 8, sts 9 and 10 in front of sts 11 and 12, sts 13 and 14 in front of sts 15 and 16 and sts 17 and 18 in front of sts 19 and 20, K 4 rows. Rep from *.

96 BACK

Machines with ribber

With ribber in position and carriage at right, set machine for 1×1 rib. Push 52 [59, 66] Ns at left and right of centre 0 to WP. 104 [118, 132] Ns. Push corresponding Ns on ribber to WP. Arrange Ns for 1×1 rib. Using MT, cast on and K 3 tubular rows. Carriage is at right. Set carriage for 1×1 rib knitting. Set RC at 000. Using MT-4/MT-4, K 10 rows. Transfer sts for st st.

Machines without ribber

Push 52 [58, 66] Ns at left and 52 [58, 65] Ns at right of centre 0 to WP. 104 [116, 131] Ns. Push every 3rd N back to NWP. Using MT and WY, cast on and K a few rows ending with carriage at left. Set RC at 000. Using MT-4 and MY, K 21 rows. Push Ns from NWP to WP and make a hem by placing loops of first row worked in MY evenly along the row. Unravel WY when work is completed.

2nd size Inc 1 st at each end.
3rd size Inc 1 st at right edge.
All sizes 104 [118, 132] sts.

All machines

Set RC at 000. Using MT, K 3 rows. Inc 1 st at each end of next and every foll 4th row until there are 126 [140, 154] sts *.
K 24 rows. RC shows 68 and work measures 18 cm, 7 in.
Shape armholes Cast off (bind off) 10 [12, 14] sts at beg of next 2 rows. Dec 1 st (2 sts in) at each end of every foll alt row until 88 [96, 104] sts rem. K 48 [52, 54] rows.
Shape neck Using a length of MY, cast off (bind off) centre 50 [58, 66] sts. Using nylon cord, K 19 sts at left by hand taking Ns down to NWP. Cont on rem sts for first side.
K 1 row. Dec 1 st (2 sts in) at beg of next and every foll alt row until 9 sts rem. K 4 rows. Using WY, K a few rows and release from machine.

With carriage at left, unravel nylon cord over rem Ns bringing Ns back to WP. Finish to correspond with first side reversing shapings.

FRONT

Work as for back to *.
Cont in cable patt, K 24 rows. RC shows 68 and work measures 18 cm, 7 in.
Shape armholes Cast off (bind off) 10 [12, 14] sts at beg of next 2 rows. Dec 1 st (2 sts in) at each end of every foll alt row until 88 [96, 104] sts rem. K 6 [10, 12] rows.
Shape neck Using a length of MY, cast off (bind off) centre 36 [44, 52] sts. Using nylon cord, K 26 sts at left by hand taking Ns down to NWP. Cont on rem sts for first side. K 1 row. Dec 1 st (2 sts in) at neck edge on next and every foll 3rd row until 9 sts rem. K 16 rows. Using WY, K a few rows and release from machine.
With carriage at left, unravel nylon cord over rem Ns bringing Ns back to WP. Finish to correspond with first side reversing shapings.

TO JOIN RIGHT SHOULDER

Push 9 Ns to WP. With K side of right back shoulder facing, replace sts on to Ns. Unravel WY. With P side of right front shoulder facing, replace sts on to same Ns. Unravel WY. Using MT and MY, K 1 row. Cast off (bind off).

TO JOIN LEFT SHOULDER

Work as for right shoulder but read left for right.

BACK NECKBAND

Machines with ribber

With ribber in position and carriage at right,

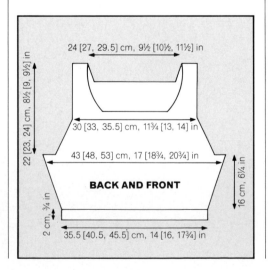

24 [27, 29.5] cm, 9½ [10½, 11½] in

22 [23, 24] cm, 8½ [9, 9½] in

30 [33, 35.5] cm, 11¾ [13, 14] in

43 [48, 53] cm, 17 [18¾, 20¾] in

BACK AND FRONT

16 cm, 6¼ in

2 cm, ¾ in

35.5 [40.5, 45.5] cm, 14 [16, 17¾] in

set machine for 1×1 rib. Using MY, cast on 87 [95, 103] sts in 1×1 rib.
* K 3 tubular rows. Carriage is at right. Set carriage for 1×1 rib knitting. Set RC at 000. Using MT-4/MT-4, K 6 rows. Transfer sts for st st *.

Machines without ribber

Push 89 [98, 107] Ns to WP.
* Push every 3rd N back to NWP. Using MT and WY, cast on and K a few rows ending with carriage at left. Set RC at 000. Using MT-4 and MY, K 15 rows. Push Ns from NWP to WP and make a hem by placing loops of first row worked in MY evenly along the row. Unravel WY when work is completed *.

All machines

With P side facing, pick up sts around back neck edge and place on to Ns. Using MT and MY, K 1 row. Cast off (bind off).

FRONT NECKBAND

Machines with ribber

With ribber in position and carriage at right, set machine for 1×1 rib. Using MY, cast on 143 [151, 159] sts in 1×1 rib. Work as for back neckband from * to *.

Machines without ribber

Push 143 [152, 161] Ns to WP. Work as for back neckband from * to *.

All machines

With P side facing, pick up sts around front neck edge and place on to Ns. Using MT and MY, K 1 row. Cast off (bind off).

ARMHOLE BANDS

Machines with ribber

With ribber in position and carriage at right, set machine for 1×1 rib. Using MY, cast on 155 [167, 179] sts in 1×1 rib. Work as for back neckband from * to *.

Machines without ribber

Push 155 [167, 179] Ns to WP. Work as for back neckband from * to *.

All machines

With P side facing, pick up sts around armhole edge and place on to Ns. Using MT and MY, K 1 row. Cast off (bind off).

PRESSING

With wrong side facing, pin out pieces to measurements given. Press carefully following instructions on cone band.

MAKING UP

Join side, neckband and armhole band seams.

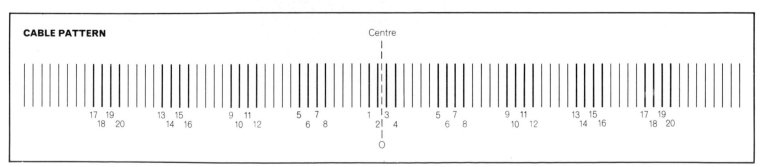

CABLE PATTERN

Centre

17 19   13 15   9 11   5 7   1 3   5 7   9 11   13 15   17 19
18 20   14 16   10 12   6 8   2 4   6 8   10 12   14 16   18 20

O

Tea Rose Cardigan

This traditional cardigan with pockets and small
neat ribs also has three rows of cables running down the
centre back. Glass buttons enhance its antique feel.

PATTERN RATING
●● Fairly easy, for knitters with some
experience.

MACHINES
This pattern is suitable for standard gauge
machines.

MATERIALS
Rowan Mulberry Silk.
525 [550, 575] g (19 [20, 21] oz) in shade 873
(MY).
5 buttons.

YARN THICKNESS
Medium heavy yarn.

MEASUREMENTS
To fit chest 76-82 [87-92, 97-102] cm, 30-32
[34-36, 38-40] in.
Actual measurement 98 [109, 120] cm, 38½
[43, 47¼] in.
Length to shoulder 56.5 [58, 59.5] cm, 22½
[22¾, 23¼] in.
Sleeve seam 50 cm, 19¾ in.
*Instructions are written for the smallest size,
larger sizes follow in square brackets. If only
one figure is given, it applies to all sizes.*

TENSION
29 stitches and 42 rows to 10 cm, 4 in
measured over stocking stitch (tension dial
setting approximately 7).
*For perfect results, your tension must be
matched exactly before starting the
garment.*

ABBREVIATIONS
See page 9.

NOTES
Knit side of knitting is right side of finished
garment.

CABLE PATTERN
Cross sts 1 and 2 in front of sts 3 and 4, K 4
rows. Cross sts 1 and 2 in front of sts 3 and
4, K 4 rows.
* Cross sts 1 and 2 in front of sts 3 and 4
and sts 5 and 6 in front of sts 7 and 8, K 4
rows. Rep from *.

BACK
Machines with ribber
With ribber in position and carriage at right,

98

set machine for 1×1 rib. Push 63 [71, 79] Ns at left and right of centre 0 to WP. 126 [142, 158] Ns.

* Push corresponding Ns on ribber to WP. Arrange Ns for 1×1 rib. Using MY, cast on and K 3 tubular rows. Carriage is at right. Set carriage for 1×1 rib knitting. Set RC at 000. Using MT-4/MT-4, K 32 rows. Transfer sts for st st *.

Machines without ribber
Push 63 [70, 79] Ns at left and 62 [70, 79] Ns at right of centre 0 to WP. 125 [140, 158] Ns.
* Push every 3rd N back to NWP. Using MT and WY, cast on and K a few rows ending with carriage at left. Set RC at 000. Using MT-4 and MY, K 61 rows. Push Ns from NWP to WP and make a hem by placing loops of first row worked in MY evenly along the row. Unravel WY when work is completed *.

1st size Inc 1 st at right edge.
2nd size Inc 1 st at each end.
All sizes 126 [142, 158] sts.
All machines
Set RC at 000. Using MT, K 11 rows. Inc 1 st at each end of next and every foll 12th row until there are 136 [152, 168] sts. Cont in cable patt. Cont to inc on every 12th row from previous inc until there are 144 [160, 176] sts. K 4 rows. RC shows 112 and work measures 33 cm, 13 in.
Shape armholes Cast off (bind off) 12 sts at beg of next 2 rows. 120 [136, 152] sts. K 92 [98, 104] rows.
Shape neck Using a length of MY, cast off (bind off) centre 58 [60, 62] sts. Using nylon cord, K 31 [38, 45] sts at left by hand taking Ns down to NWP. Cont on rem sts for first side.
K 1 row. Dec 1 st at beg of next and foll alt

Wear the Tea Rose Cardigan together with the Cabled Silk top and Silk Skirt to make an elegant outfit.

row. 29 [36, 43] sts. K 2 rows. Using WY, K a few rows and release from machine. With carriage at left, unravel nylon cord over rem Ns bringing Ns back to WP. Finish to correspond with first side reversing shapings.

RIGHT FRONT
Machines with ribber
With ribber in position and carriage at right, set machine for 1×1 rib. Push 31 [35, 39] Ns at left and right of centre 0 to WP. 62 [70, 78] Ns. Work as for back from * to *.
Machines without ribber
Push 31 [34, 39] Ns at left and 31 [34, 38] Ns at right of centre 0 to WP. 62 [68, 77] Ns. Work as for back from * to *.
2nd size Inc 1 st at each end.
3rd size Inc 1 st at right edge.
All sizes 62 [70, 78] sts.
All machines
Set RC at 000. Using MT, K 11 rows. Inc 1 st at right edge (left edge on left front) on next and every foll 12th row until there are 67 [75, 83] sts. Cont in cable patt. Cont to inc on every 12th row from previous inc until there are 71 [79, 87] sts. K 4 rows. RC shows 112 and work measures 33 cm, 13 in. K 1 row extra for left front only.
Shape armhole Cast off (bind off) 12 sts at beg of next row. 59 [67, 75] sts. K 66 [72, 78] rows.
Shape neck Cast off (bind off) 16 sts at beg of next row. Dec 1 st (2 sts in) at neck edge on every row until 29 [36, 43] sts rem. K 18 [17, 16] rows. Using WY, K a few rows in st st and release from machine.

LEFT FRONT
Work as for right front reversing shapings by noting alteration in number of rows worked.

POCKETS
Push 28 Ns to WP. Using MT and WY, cast on and K a few rows ending with carriage at right. Using MY, K 30 rows. Using WY, K a few rows and release from machine.

POCKET TOPS
Machines with ribber
With ribber in position and carriage at right, set machine for 1×1 rib. Using MY, cast on 28 sts in 1×1 rib. K 3 tubular rows. Carriage is at right. Set carriage for 1×1 rib knitting. Set RC at 000. Using MT-4/MT-4, K 6 rows. Transfer sts for st st.
Machines without ribber
Push 29 Ns to WP. Push every 3rd N back to NWP. Using MT and WY, cast on and K a few rows ending with carriage at left. Set RC at 000. Using MT-4 and MY, K 15 rows. Push Ns from NWP to WP and make a hem by placing loops of first row worked in MY evenly along the row.
Unravel WY when work is completed. Dec 1 st. 28 sts.

All machines
With P side facing, replace 28 sts from last row of pocket on to Ns. Using MT and MY, K 1 row. Cast off (bind off).

SLEEVES
Machines with ribber
With ribber in position and carriage at right, set machine for 1×1 rib. Push 29 [32, 35] Ns at left and right of centre 0 to WP. 58 [64, 70] Ns. Work as for back from * to *.

Machines without ribber
Push 28 [31, 34] Ns at left and right of centre 0 to WP. 56 [62, 68] Ns. Work as for back from * to *. Inc 1 st at each end. 58 [64, 70] sts.

All machines
Set RC at 000. Using MT, K 3 rows. Inc 1 st at each end of next and every foll 4th row until there are 138 [146, 154] sts. K 24 [20, 16] rows. RC shows 184 and work measures 50 cm, 19¾ in. Place marker at each end. K 18 rows. Using WY, K a few rows and release from machine.

TO JOIN RIGHT SHOULDER
Push 29 [36, 43] Ns to WP. With K side of right back shoulder facing, replace sts on to Ns. Unravel WY. With P side of right front shoulder facing, replace sts on to same Ns. Unravel WY. Using MT and MY, K 1 row. Cast off (bind off).

TO JOIN LEFT SHOULDER
Work as given for the right shoulder but read left instead of right.

NECKBAND
Machines with ribber
With ribber in position and carriage at right, set machine for 1×1 rib. Using MY, cast on 150 [154, 158] sts in 1×1 rib. K 3 tubular rows. Carriage is at right. Set carriage for 1×1 rib knitting. Set RC at 000. Using MT-4/MT-4, K 18 rows. Transfer sts for st st.

Machines without ribber
Push 149 [155, 161] Ns to WP. Push every 3rd N back to NWP. Using MT and WY, cast on and K a few rows ending with carriage at left. Set RC at 000. Using MT-4 and MY, K 21 rows. Push Ns from NWP to WP and make a hem by placing loops of first row worked in MY evenly along the row. Unravel WY when work is completed.

All machines
With P side facing, pick up sts around neck edge and place on to Ns. Using MT and MY, K 1 row. Cast off (bind off).

Machines with ribber
Fold neckband in half to inside and slipstitch down.

BUTTONHOLE BAND
Machines with ribber
With ribber in position and carriage at right, set machine for 1×1 rib. Using MY, cast on 150 [154, 158] sts in 1×1 rib. K 3 tubular rows. Carriage is at right. Set carriage for 1×1 rib knitting. Set RC at 000. Using MT-4/MT-4, K 4 rows. Counting from right edge, make buttonholes over sts 5, 6; 39, 40; 75, 76; 111, 112; 145 and 146 [5, 6; 41, 42; 77, 78; 113, 114; 149 and 150, 5, 6; 41, 42; 79, 80; 117, 118; 153 and 154]. K 11 rows. Make buttonholes over same Ns as before. K 4 rows. Transfer sts for st st.

Machines without ribber
Push 150 [154, 158] Ns to WP. Using MT and WY, cast on and K a few rows ending with carriage at right. Set RC at 000. Using MT-1 and MY, K 4 rows. Counting from right edge, make buttonholes over sts 5, 6; 39, 40; 75, 76; 111, 112; 145 and 146 [5, 6; 41, 42; 77, 78; 113, 114; 149 and 150, 5, 6; 41, 42; 79, 80; 117, 118; 153 and 154]. K 9 rows. Make buttonholes over same Ns as before. K 4 rows. Make a hem by placing loops of first row worked in MY on to corresponding Ns. Unravel WY when work is completed.

All machines
With P side facing, pick up sts along right front edge and place on to Ns. Using MT and MY, K 1 row. Cast off (bind off).

BUTTON BAND
Work as for buttonhole band omitting buttonholes and reading left front for right front.

TO JOIN SLEEVES TO ARMHOLES
Push 138 [146, 154] Ns to WP. With K side of sleeve facing, replace 138 [146, 154] sts on to Ns. Unravel WY. With P side facing, pick up 138 [146, 154] sts along side edge of armhole and place on to same Ns. Using MT and MY, K 1 row. Cast off (bind off).

PRESSING
With wrong side facing, pin out pieces to measurements given. Press carefully following instructions on cone band.

MAKING UP
Sew rows above markers on sleeves to cast off (bound off) sts on back and front. Join side and sleeve seams. Graft lower edge of pockets into position. Sew side edges into position.

Machines with ribber
Fold front bands in half to inside and slipstitch down.

All machines
Neaten open ends of bands. Finish buttonholes. Sew on buttons.

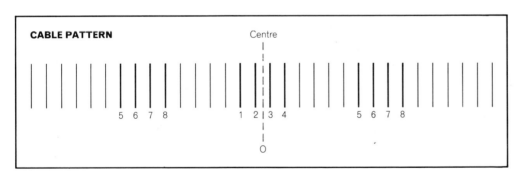

CABLE PATTERN

Centre

5 6 7 8   1 2 3 4   5 6 7 8

0

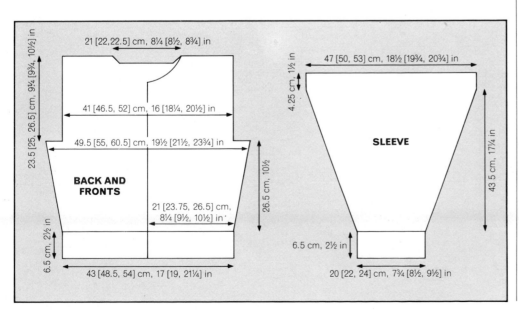

21 [22, 22.5] cm, 8¼ [8½, 8¾] in

23.5 [25, 26.5] cm, 9¼ [9¾, 10½] in

41 [46.5, 52] cm, 16 [18¼, 20½] in

49.5 [55, 60.5] cm, 19½ [21½, 23¾] in

BACK AND FRONTS

21 [23.75, 26.5] cm, 8¼ [9½, 10½] in

6.5 cm, 2½ in

43 [48.5, 54] cm, 17 [19, 21¼] in

47 [50, 53] cm, 18½ [19¾, 20¾] in

4.25 cm, 1½ in

SLEEVE

26.5 cm, 10½

43.5 cm, 17¼ in

6.5 cm, 2½ in

20 [22, 24] cm, 7¾ [8½, 9½] in

Silk Skirt

This slender skirt is simple to make. The length can be altered by adding or omitting rows. It could also be worn with the Tea Rose Cardigan.

100

PATTERN RATING
●● Fairly easy, for knitters with some experience.

MACHINES
This pattern is suitable for standard gauge machines.

MATERIALS
Rowan Mulberry Silk.
275 [300, 325] g (10 [11, 12] oz) in shade 870 (MY).
Elastic to fit waist.

YARN THICKNESS
Medium heavy yarn.

MEASUREMENTS
Length 47 cm, 18½ in.

TENSION
29 stitches and 42 rows to 10 cm, 4 in measured over stocking stitch (tension dial setting approximately 7).
For perfect results, your tension must be matched exactly before starting the garment.

ABBREVIATIONS
See page 9.

NOTES
Knit side of knitting is right side of finished garment.

Machines with ribber
With ribber in position and carriage at right, set machine for 1×1 rib. Using MY, cast on 132 [148, 164] sts in 1×1 rib. K 3 tubular rows. Carriage is at right. Set carriage for 1×1 rib knitting. Set RC at 000. Using MT-4/MT-4, K 12 rows. Transfer sts for st st.
Machines without ribber
Push 131 [146, 164] Ns to WP. Push every 3rd N back to NWP. Using MT and WY, cast on and K a few rows ending with carriage at left. Set RC at 000. Using MT-4 and MY, K 25 rows. Push Ns from NWP to WP and make a hem by placing loops of first row worked in MY evenly along the row. Unravel WY when work is completed.
1st size Inc 1 st at right edge.
2nd size Inc 1 st at each end.
All sizes 132 [148, 164] sts.

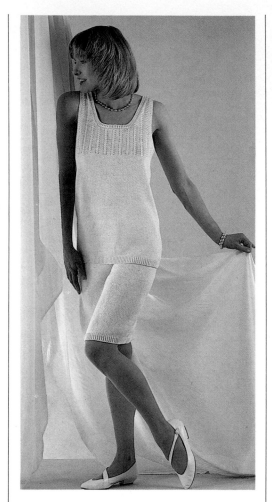

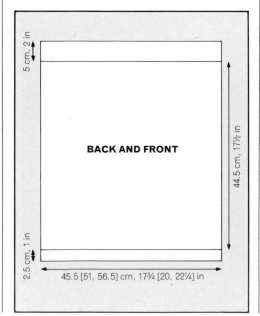

5 cm, 2 in

44.5 cm, 17½ in

BACK AND FRONT

2.5 cm, 1 in

45.5 [51, 56.5] cm, 17¾ [20, 22¼] in

All machines
Set RC at 000. Using MT, K 188 rows. Work measures 47 cm, 18½ in.
Machines without ribber
1st size Dec 1 st at right edge.
2nd size Dec 1 st at each end.
All sizes 131 [146, 164] sts.
All machines
Using WY, K a few rows and release from machine.

WAISTBAND (Two pieces)
Machines with ribber
With ribber in position and carriage at right, set machine for 1×1 rib. Using MY, cast on 132 [148, 164] sts in 1×1 rib. K 3 tubular rows. Carriage is at right. Set carriage for 1×1 rib knitting. Set RC at 000. Using MT-4/MT-4, K 50 rows. Transfer sts for st st.
Machines without ribber
Push 131 [146, 164] Ns to WP. Push every 3rd N back to NWP. Using MT and WY, cast on and K a few rows ending with carriage at left. Set RC at 000. Using MT-4 and MY, K 49 rows. Push Ns from NWP to WP and make a hem by placing loops of first row worked in MY evenly along the row. Unravel WY when work is completed.
All machines
With P side facing, pick up sts from top of skirt and place on to Ns. Using MT and MY, K 1 row. Cast off (bind off).

PRESSING
With wrong side facing, pin out pieces to measurements given. Press carefully following instructions on cone band.

MAKING UP
Machines with ribber
Join side and waistband seams. Fold waistband in half to inside and slipstitch down, leaving a small opening. Insert elastic and join ends.
Machines without ribber
Join side and waistband seams, leaving a small opening in waistband. Insert elastic and join ends.

Cabled Silk

A simple top with a series of narrow cables around the neck. Worn on its own or with the skirt, it is easily made in a beautiful silk yarn.

PATTERN RATING

● ● Fairly easy, for knitters with some experience.

MACHINES

This pattern is suitable for standard gauge machines.

MATERIALS

Rowan Mulberry Silk.
225 [250, 275] g (8 [9, 10] oz) in shade 870 (MY).

YARN THICKNESS

Medium heavy yarn.

MEASUREMENTS

To fit chest 76-82 [87-92, 97-102] cm, 30-32 [34-36, 38-40] in.
Actual measurement 88 [98, 108] cm, 34¾ [38½, 42½] in.
Length to shoulder 63.5 [64.5, 65.5] cm, 25 [25¼, 25¾] in.
Instructions are written for the smallest size, larger sizes follow in square brackets. If only one figure is given, it applies to all sizes.

TENSION

29 stitches and 42 rows to 10 cm, 4 in measured over stocking stitch (tension dial setting approximately 7).
31 stitches and 48 rows to 10 cm, 4 in measured over cable pattern (tension dial setting approximately 7).
For perfect results, your tension must be matched exactly before starting the garment.

ABBREVIATIONS

See page 9.

NOTES

Knit side of knitting is right side of finished garment.

CABLE PATTERN

* Cross sts 1 and 2 in front of sts 3 and 4. K 4 rows. Rep from *.

BACK

Machines with ribber

With ribber in position and carriage at right, set machine for 1×1 rib. Push 69 [77, 85] Ns at left and right of centre 0 to WP. 138 [154, 170] Ns. Push corresponding Ns on ribber to

WP. Arrange Ns for 1×1 rib. Using MY, cast on and K 3 tubular rows. Carriage is at right. Set carriage for 1×1 rib knitting. Set RC at 000. Using MT-4/MT-4, K 12 rows. Transfer sts for st st.

Machines without ribber

Push 69 [76, 85] Ns at left and 68 [76, 85] Ns at right of centre 0 to WP. 137 [152, 170] Ns. Push every 3rd N back to NWP. Using MT and WY, cast on and K a few rows ending

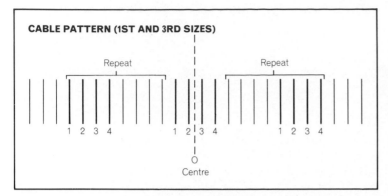

CABLE PATTERN (1ST AND 3RD SIZES)

Repeat   Repeat

1 2 3 4   1 2 3 4   1 2 3 4

O
Centre

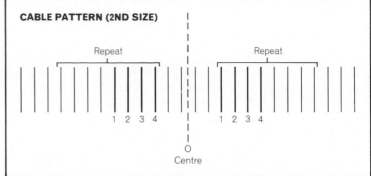

CABLE PATTERN (2ND SIZE)

Repeat   Repeat

1 2 3 4   1 2 3 4

O
Centre

102

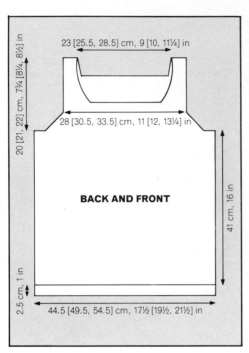

23 [25.5, 28.5] cm, 9 [10, 11¼] in

20 [21, 22] cm, 7¾ [8¼, 8½] in

28 [30.5, 33.5] cm, 11 [12, 13¼] in

BACK AND FRONT

41 cm, 16 in

2.5 cm, 1 in

44.5 [49.5, 54.5] cm, 17½ [19½, 21½] in

with carriage at left. Set RC at 000. Using MT-4 and MY, K 25 rows. Push Ns from NWP to WP and make a hem by placing loops of first row worked in MY evenly along the row. Unravel WY when work is completed.
1st size Inc 1 st at right edge.
2nd size Inc 1 st at each end.
All sizes 138 [154, 170] sts.
All machines
Set RC at 000. Using MT, K 156 rows. Cont in cable patt, K 18 rows. RC shows 174 and work measures 43.5 cm, 17¼ in.
Shape armholes Cast off (bind off) 14 [16, 18] sts at beg of next 2 rows. Dec 1 st (2 sts in) at each end of every foll alt row until 88 [96, 104] sts rem *.
K 48 [50, 50] rows.
Shape neck Using a length of MY, cast off (bind off) centre 50 [58, 66] sts. Using nylon cord, K 19 sts at left by hand taking Ns down to NWP. Cont on rem sts for first side.
K 1 row. Dec 1 st (2 sts in) at beg of next and every foll alt row until 8 sts rem. K 2 rows. Using WY, K a few rows in st st and release from machine.
With carriage at left, unravel nylon cord over rem Ns bringing Ns back to WP. Finish to correspond with first side reversing shapings.

FRONT
Work as for back to *. K 8 [10, 10] rows.

Shape neck Using a length of MY, cast off (bind off) centre 36 [44, 52] sts. Using nylon cord, K 26 sts at left by hand taking Ns down to NWP. Cont on rem sts for first side. K 1 row. Dec 1 st (2 sts in) at neck edge on next and every foll 3rd row until 8 sts rem. K 11 rows. Using WY, K a few rows in st st and release from machine.
With carriage at left, unravel nylon cord over rem Ns bringing Ns back to WP. Finish to correspond with first side reversing shapings.

TO JOIN RIGHT SHOULDER
Push 8 Ns to WP. With K side of right back shoulder facing, replace sts on to Ns. Unravel WY. With P side of right front shoulder facing, replace sts on to same Ns. Unravel WY. Using MT and MY, K 1 row. Cast off (bind off).

TO JOIN LEFT SHOULDER
Work as for right shoulder but read left for right.

BACK NECKBAND
Machines with ribber
With ribber in position and carriage at right, set machine for 1×1 rib. Using MY, cast on 87 [95, 103] sts in 1×1 rib.
* K 3 tubular rows. Carriage is at right. Set carriage for 1×1 rib knitting. Set RC at 000. Using MT-4/MT-4, K 6 rows. Transfer sts for st st *.

Machines without ribber
Push 89 [98, 107] Ns to WP.
* Push every 3rd N back to NWP. Using MT and WY, cast on and K a few rows ending with carriage at left. Set RC at 000. Using MT-4 and MY, K 15 rows. Push Ns from NWP to WP and make a hem by placing loops of first row worked in MY evenly along the row. Unravel WY when work is completed *.

All machines
With P side facing, pick up sts around back neck edge and place on to Ns. Using MT and MY, K 1 row. Cast off (bind off).

FRONT NECKBAND
Machines with ribber
With ribber in position and carriage at right, set machine for 1×1 rib. Using MY, cast on 143 [151, 159] sts in 1×1 rib.
Now work as given for the back neckband from * to *.

Machines without ribber
Push 143 [152, 161] Ns to WP. Work as for back neckband from * to *.
All machines
With P side facing, pick up sts around front neck edge and place on to Ns. Using MT and MY, K 1 row. Cast off (bind off).

ARMHOLE BANDS
Machines with ribber
With ribber in position and carriage at right, set machine for 1×1 rib. Using MY, cast on 155 [167, 179] sts in 1×1 rib. Work as for back neckband from * to *.
Machines without ribber
Push 155 [167, 179] Ns to WP. Work as for back neckband from * to *.
All machines
With P side facing, pick up sts around armhole edge and place on to Ns. Using MT and MY, K 1 row. Cast off (bind off).

PRESSING
With wrong side facing, pin out pieces to measurements given. Press carefully following instructions on cone band.

MAKING UP
Join side, neckband and armhole band seams.

Metropolitan

The use of silk and wool mixed yarn gives this sweater/dress an interesting surface. It works best in fairly neutral colours using different shades of the same colour.

PATTERN RATING
● Easy to knit.

MACHINES
This pattern is suitable for standard gauge machines.

MATERIALS
Any yarn that has a slub in order to add texture and keep it light.
600 g (22 oz) in navy or dark cream (MC).
300 g (11 oz) in blue or light cream (C).
The yarn used is 80% Wool, 20% Silk.

YARN THICKNESS
Medium yarn with two strands used together.

MEASUREMENTS
To fit chest 87-97 cm, 34-38 in.
Actual measurement 156 cm, 61½ in.
Length to shoulder 91.5 cm, 36 in.
Sleeve seam 44 cm, 17¼ in.

TENSION
24 stitches and 32 rows to 10 cm, 4 in measured over stocking stitch using two strands of yarn tog (tension dial setting approximately 10).
For perfect results, your tension must be matched exactly before starting the garment.

ABBREVIATIONS
See page 9.

NOTES
Knit side of knitting is right side of finished garment.
Two strands of yarn are used together throughout.

BACK
Machines with ribber
With ribber in position and carriage at right, set machine for 1×1 rib. Using MC, cast on 142 sts in 1×1 rib. K 3 tubular rows. Carriage is at right. Set carriage for 1×1 rib knitting. Set RC at 000. Using MT-7/MT-7, K 10 rows. Using MT/MT, K 34 rows. Transfer sts for st st.
Machines without ribber
Push 140 Ns to WP. Push every 3rd N back to NWP. Using MT and WY, cast on and K a few rows ending with carriage at left. Set RC

at 000. Using MC, K 34 rows. Using MT-5, K 21 rows. Using MT, K 34 rows. Push Ns from NWP to WP and make a hem by placing loops of first row worked in MC evenly along the row. Unravel WY when work is completed. Inc 2 sts. 142 sts.

All machines
Set RC at 000. Using MT and C, K 4 rows. Shape sides by inc 1 st at each end of next and every foll 5th row until there are 190 sts. K 4 rows. RC shows 124 and work measures 51.5 cm, 20¼ in.
Shape armholes Cast off (bind off) 40 sts at beg of next 2 rows. 110 sts **.
K 114 rows.
Shape neck Using a length of C, cast off (bind off) centre 52 sts. Push 29 Ns at left to HP or knit on to WY, if preferred, and cont on rem sts for first side.
K 1 row. Dec 1 st at beg of next and foll alt row. 27 sts. K 8 rows. Using WY, K a few rows and release from machine.
With carriage at left, push rem Ns from HP to UWP and finish to correspond with first side reversing shapings.

FRONT
Work as for back to *.
Shape neck Using a length of C, cast off (bind off) centre 26 sts. Push 42 Ns at left to HP and cont on rem sts for first side.
K 5 rows. Dec 1 st (3 sts in) at neck edge on next and every foll 8th row until 27 sts rem. K 8 rows. Using WY, K a few rows and release from machine.
With carriage at left, push rem Ns from HP to UWP and finish to correspond with first side reversing shapings.

SLEEVES
Machines with ribber
With ribber in position and carriage at right, set machine for 1×1 rib. Using MC, cast on 90 sts in 1×1 rib. K 3 tubular rows. Carriage is at right. Set carriage for 1×1 rib knitting. Set RC at 000. Using MT-7/MT-7, K 10 rows. Using MT-4/MT-4, K 24 rows. Transfer sts for st st.
Machines without ribber
Push 89 Ns to WP. Push every 3rd N back to NWP. Using MT and WY, cast on and K a few rows ending with carriage at left. Set RC at 000. Using MT-2 and MC, K 24 rows. Using MT-5, K 21 rows. Using MT-2, K 24 rows. Push Ns from NWP to WP and make a hem by placing loops of first row worked in MC evenly along the row. Unravel WY when work is completed. Inc 1 st. 90 sts.
All machines
Set RC at 000. Using MT, K 1 row. Shape sides by inc 1 st at each end of next and every foll alt row until there are 192 sts. K 4 rows. RC shows 106 and work measures 44 cm, 17¼ in. Place marker at each end. K 54 rows. Using WY, K a few rows and release from machine.

COLLAR (Two pieces)
Using MC, cast on 122 sts by hand. Set RC

at 000. Using MT, K 100 rows. Cast off (bind off).

TO JOIN RIGHT SHOULDER
Push 27 Ns to WP. With K side of right back shoulder facing, replace sts on to Ns. Unravel WY. With P side of right front shoulder facing, replace sts on to same Ns. Unravel WY. Using MT and C, K 1 row. Cast off (bind off).

TO JOIN LEFT SHOULDER
Work as for right shoulder, reading left for right.

TO JOIN SLEEVES TO ARMHOLES
Push 192 Ns to WP. With K side facing, replace 192 sts from top of sleeve on to Ns. Unravel WY. With P side facing, pick up 192 sts along side edge of armhole and place on to same Ns. Using MT and MC, K 1 row. Cast off (bind off).

PRESSING
With wrong side facing, pin out to measurements given. Press carefully following instructions on cone band.

MAKING UP
Sew rows above markers on sleeve to cast off (bound off) sts on back and front. Join sleeve and side seams, leaving welts open. Join centre back seam in collar. Fold collar lengthways and lightly steam. Sew collar into position, lapping right over left and easing in ends.

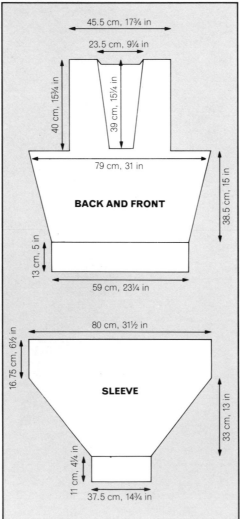

45.5 cm, 17¾ in

23.5 cm, 9¼ in

40 cm, 15¾ in

39 cm, 15¼ in

79 cm, 31 in

BACK AND FRONT

38.5 cm, 15 in

13 cm, 5 in

59 cm, 23¼ in

80 cm, 31½ in

16.75 cm, 6½ in

SLEEVE

33 cm, 13 in

11 cm, 4¼ in

37.5 cm, 14¾ in

104

Winter Classics

Very simple motifs, like squares or oakleaves, create quite timeless patterns. There are many diverse and easily recognizable leaf shapes which could be given a similar half-shading treatment, and triangles or diamonds would be interesting alternatives to the square.

The 1951 Festival of Britain formed the basis for the Fair Isle Oak Leaf pattern. The small dots or stitches between the leaves solve the problem of large floats across the back and also provide a graphic link with the style of that period. The sleeveless cardigan has a plain back with an optional half belt and two small pockets on the front. The trimming ribs are deliberately very thin so that, with the close patterning repeat of the oakleaf, a brocade effect is produced. It is worth experimenting by swapping colours around so that the positive colour of the leaf becomes the background, as in the two versions of the Squares design.

The Squares design offers two alternatives: the man's sweater and the cropped woman's version with shorter sleeves. Remember, you can always interchange the sleeves pattern to make a long woman's sweater. Both versions have randomly selected squares in different colours. The number of squares and colour combinations selected is entirely up to the individual, but I think the design is most successful if the squares are positioned with economy so that there is an element of discovery when the viewer looks at it. If you want to adapt the Squares Fair Isle pattern for a child's version, scale down the square or reduce the stitch/row interval.

The Oak Leaf sleeveless cardigan and the two Squares sweaters are knitted with a flecked yarn which gives the patterns an added surface interest. They also work successfully with plain yarn, and brighter colours can suggest a more contemporary feel. Squares, Short Squares and the Oak Leaf design are also adaptable for spring sweaters simply by changing the colours or by using a cotton yarn, provided of course the tensions match.

In common with many of the designs in this book, the oakleaf itself could be isolated and enlarged as a motif for a child's sweater, or perhaps used only as a yoke detail, the rest of the sweater just being Fair Isled with dots. Surprisingly, often very small changes in colour, yarn and scale alter a design radically, so it is a good idea to knit a swatch first before embarking on the actual item.

Squares

A simple, effective pattern using
flecked wool. Random squares
are selected in different colours.

PATTERN RATING
● ● ● For fairly experienced knitters.

MACHINES
This pattern is suitable for standard gauge
machines.

MATERIALS
Rowan Fine Fleck Tweed.
425 g (15 oz) in shade 82 (MC).
65 g (3 oz) in shade 99 (C).
Oddments in shade 77, shade 39 and
shade 54.
*Rowan Fine Fleck Tweed is 75% Pure New
Wool base, 15% Cotton Nepp, 10% Nylon.*

YARN THICKNESS
Medium yarn.

MEASUREMENTS
To fit chest 102 cm, 40 in.
Actual measurement 125 cm, 49¼ in.
Length to shoulder 67 cm, 26½ in.
Sleeve seam 52.5 cm, 20¾ in.

TENSION
28.5 stitches and 38.5 rows to 10 cm, 4 in
measured over Fair Isle pattern (tension dial
setting approximately 7).
*For perfect results, your tension must be
matched exactly before starting the
garment.*

ABBREVIATIONS
See page 9.

NOTES
Knit side of knitting is right side of finished
garment.
Punchcard machines
The card shown on page 108 should be
punched, if required, before starting to knit.
Electronic machines
Fill in pattern card, if required, before
starting to knit.
Two colour Fair Isle rows should be knitted
with the first colour given in the back feeder
1(A) to knit the background and the second
colour given in the front feeder 2(B) to knit
the contrast pattern.

*The darker background colour chosen for
the woman's sweater makes the random
coloured squares look brighter than in the
man's Squares sweater.*

FAIR ISLE PATTERN
K 12 rows MC only (st st) and 4 rows MC/C.
These 16 rows form patt repeat.
To add an odd different colour square:-
Push Ns for selected square to HP just after
12 st st rows. K Fair Isle row, then K sts in
HP by hand with a length of a different
colour (hooking yarn over adjacent Ns in
WP). After knitting by hand, push Ns back to
HP and repeat for next 3 rows.

BACK
Machines with ribber
With ribber in position and carriage at right,
set machine for 1×1 rib. Push 84 Ns at left
and right of centre 0 to WP. 168 Ns.
* Push corresponding Ns on ribber to WP.
Arrange Ns for 1×1 rib. Using MC, cast on
and K 3 tubular rows. Carriage is at right.
Insert card and lock on first row. Set
carriage for 1×1 rib knitting. Set RC at 000.
Using MT-6/MT-6, K 12 rows. Transfer sts for
st st *.
Machines without ribber
Push 84 Ns at left and 83 Ns at right of
centre 0 to WP. 167 Ns.
* Push every 3rd N back to NWP. Using MT
and WY, cast on and K a few rows ending
with carriage at left. Insert card and lock on
first row. Set RC at 000. Using MT-2 and
MC, K 19 rows. Push Ns from NWP to WP
and make a hem by placing loops of first

row worked in MC evenly along the row.
Unravel WY when work is completed *.
Inc 1 st at right edge. 168 sts.
All machines
Release card and cont in Fair Isle patt. Set
RC at 000. Using MT, K 19 rows. Shape
sides by inc 1 st at each end of next and
every foll 20th row until there are 180 sts. K
28 rows. RC shows 148 and work measures
40 cm, 15¾ in.
Shape armholes Cast off (bind off) 14 sts at
beg of next 2 rows. 152 sts **.
K 96 rows. Cont in st st and MC.
Shape neck Using a length of MC, cast off
centre 56 sts. Using nylon cord, K 48 sts at
left by hand taking Ns down to NWP. Cont
on rem sts for first side.
K 1 row. Dec 1 st at beg of next and foll alt
row. 46 sts. K 2 rows. Using WY, K a few
rows and release from machine.
With carriage at left, unravel nylon cord over
rem Ns bringing Ns back to WP. Finish to
correspond with first side reversing shapings.

FRONT
Work as for back to **. K 76 rows.
Shape neck Note patt row on card. Using a
length of MC, cast off (bind off) centre 34
sts. Using nylon cord, K 59 sts at left by
hand taking Ns down to NWP. Cont on rem
sts for first side.
K 1 row. Dec 1 st at beg of next and every foll

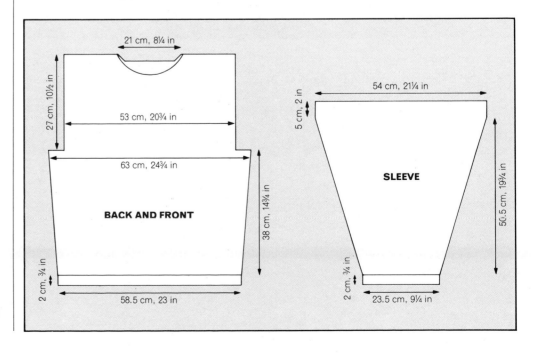

108

All machines
Release card and cont in Fair Isle patt. Set RC at 000. Using MT, shape sides by inc 1 st at each end of next and every foll 4th row until there are 154 sts. K 27 rows. RC shows 196 and work measures 52.5 cm, 20¾ in. Place marker at each end. K 19 rows. Using WY, K a few rows in st st and release from machine.

TO JOIN RIGHT SHOULDER
Push 46 Ns to WP. With K side of right back shoulder facing, replace sts on to Ns. Unravel WY. With P side of right front shoulder facing, replace sts on to same Ns. Unravel WY. Using MT and MC, K 1 row. Cast off (bind off).

NECKBAND
Machines with ribber
With ribber in position and carriage at right, set machine for 1×1 rib. Using MC, cast on 140 sts in 1×1 rib. K 3 tubular rows. Carriage is at right. Set carriage for 1×1 rib knitting. Set RC at 000. Using MT-6/MT-6, K 24 rows. Transfer sts for st st. With P side facing, pick up sts around neck edge and place on to Ns. Using MT, K 1 row. Cast off (bind off).
Machines without ribber
Push 140 Ns to WP. With K side facing, pick up 140 sts around neck edge and place on to Ns. Set RC at 000. Using MT and MC, K 1 row. Transfer every 3rd st on to adjacent N and push empty Ns to NWP. Using MT-1, K 4 rows. Using MT-2, K 11 rows. Using MT-1, K 3 rows. Push Ns from NWP to WP and place loop from row below adjacent st on to empty Ns. Using MT, K 2 rows. Using WY, K a few rows and release from machine.

TO JOIN LEFT SHOULDER
Work as for right shoulder, reading left for right.

TO JOIN SLEEVES TO ARMHOLES
Push 154 Ns to WP. With K side facing, replace 154 sts from top of sleeve on to Ns. Unravel WY. With P side facing, pick up 154 sts along side edge of armhole and place on to same Ns. Using MT and MC, K 1 row. Cast off (bind off).

PRESSING
With wrong side facing, pin out to measurements given. Press carefully following instructions on cone band.

MAKING UP
Sew rows above markers on sleeves to cast off (bound off) sts on back and front. Join side, sleeve and neckband seams.
Machines with ribber
Fold neckband in half to inside and slipstitch down.
Machines without ribber
Fold neckband in half to outside and pin in position. Unravelling WY as required, backstitch through open loops of last row worked in MC.

alt row until 46 sts rem. Using WY, K a few rows in st st and release from machine. With carriage at right, unravel nylon cord over rem Ns, bringing Ns back to WP. Lock card on number previously noted. Set carriage for patt and take to left without knitting. Release card and cont in Fair Isle patt. Finish to correspond with first side reversing shapings.

SLEEVES
Machines with ribber
With ribber in position and carriage at right, set machine for 1×1 rib. Push 34 Ns at left and right of centre 0 to WP. 68 Ns. Work as for back from * to *.
Machines without ribber
Push 34 Ns at left and right of centre 0 to WP. 68 Ns. Work as for back from * to *.

Short Squares

This is a cropped version
of the man's Squares sweater.

It is in a reverse colourway
with randomly selected squares.

PATTERN RATING
● ● ● For fairly experienced knitters.

MACHINES
This pattern is suitable for standard gauge
machines.

MATERIALS
Rowan Fine Fleck Tweed.
365 g (13 oz) in shade 97 (MC).
60 g (2 oz) in shade 82 (C).
Oddments in shade 124, shade 56, shade 44
and shade 12.
*Rowan Fine Fleck Tweed is 75% Pure New
Wool base, 15% Cotton Nepp, 10% Nylon.*

YARN THICKNESS
Medium yarn.

MEASUREMENTS
To fit bust 92 cm, 36 in.
Actual measurement 125 cm, 49¼ in.
Length to shoulder 50 cm, 19¾ in.
Sleeve seam 45.5 cm, 18 in.

TENSION
28½ stitches and 38½ rows to 10 cm, 4 in.
measured over Fair Isle pattern (tension dial
setting approximately 7).
*For perfect results, your tension must be
matched exactly before starting the
garment.*

ABBREVIATIONS
See page 9.

NOTES
Knit side of knitting is right side of finished
garment.
Punchcard machines
The card shown on page 111 should be
punched, if required, before starting to knit.
Electronic machines
Fill in pattern card, if required, before
starting to knit.
Two colour Fair Isle rows should be knitted
with the first colour given in the back feeder
1(A) to knit the background and the second
colour given in the front feeder 2(B) to knit
the contrast pattern.

FAIR ISLE PATTERN
K 12 rows MC only (st st) and 4 rows MC/C.
These 16 rows form patt repeat.
To add an odd different colour square:-

Push Ns for selected square to HP just after 12 st st rows. K Fair Isle row, then K sts in HP by hand with a length of a different colour (hooking yarn over adjacent Ns in WP). After knitting by hand, push Ns back to HP and repeat for next 3 rows.

BACK
Machines with ribber
With ribber in position and carriage at right, set machine for 1×1 rib. Push 84 Ns at left and right of centre 0 to WP. 168 Ns.
* Push corresponding Ns on ribber to WP. Arrange Ns for 1×1 rib. Using MC, cast on and K 3 tubular rows. Carriage is at right. Insert card and lock on first row. Set carriage for 1×1 rib knitting. Set RC at 000. Using MT-6/MT-6, K 12 rows. Transfer sts for st st *.

Machines without ribber
Push 84 Ns at left and 83 Ns at right of centre 0 to WP. 167 Ns.
* Push every 3rd N back to NWP. Using MT and WY, cast on and K a few rows ending with carriage at left. Insert card and lock on first row. Set RC at 000. Using MT-2 and MC K 19 rows. Push Ns from NWP to WP and make a hem by placing loops of first row worked in MC evenly along the row. Unravel WY when work is completed *.
Inc 1 st at right edge. 168 sts.

All machines
Release card and cont in Fair Isle patt. Set RC at 000. Using MT, K 9 rows. Shape sides by inc 1 st at each end of next and every foll 10th row until there are 180 sts. K 10 rows. RC shows 70 and work measures 20 cm, 8 in.
Shape armholes Cast off (bind off) 14 sts at beg of next 2 rows. 152 sts **.
K 108 rows. Cont in st st and MC.
Shape neck Using a length of MC, cast off (bind off) centre 56 sts. Using nylon cord, K 48 sts at left by hand taking Ns down to NWP. Cont on rem sts for first side.
K 1 row. Dec 1 st at beg of next and foll alt row. 46 sts. K 2 rows. Using WY, K a few rows and release from machine.
With carriage at left, unravel nylon cord over rem Ns bringing Ns back to WP. Finish to correspond with first side reversing shapings.

FRONT
Work as for back to **.
K 84 rows.
Shape neck Note patt row on card. Using a length of MC, cast off (bind off) centre 34 sts. Using nylon cord, K 59 sts at left by hand taking Ns down to NWP. Cont on rem sts for first side.
K 1 row. Dec 1 st at beg of next and every foll alt row until 46 sts rem. K 4 rows. Using WY, K a few rows in st st and release from machine.
With carriage at right, unravel nylon cord over rem Ns, bringing Ns back to WP. Lock card on number previously noted. Set carriage for patt and take to left without knitting. Release card and cont in Fair Isle patt. Finish to correspond with first side reversing shapings.

SLEEVES
Machines with ribber
With ribber in position and carriage at right, set machine for 1×1 rib. Push 28 Ns at left and right of centre 0 to WP. 56 Ns. Work as for back from * to *.
Machines without ribber
Push 28 Ns at left and right of centre 0 to WP. 56 Ns. Work as for back from * to *.
All machines
Release card and cont in Fair Isle patt. Set RC at 000. Using MT, shape sides by inc 1 st at each end of next and every foll 3rd row until there are 124 sts, then on every foll alt row until there are 172 sts. K 20 rows. RC shows 168 and work measures 45.5 cm, 18 in. Place marker at each end. K 19 rows. Using WY, K a few rows in st st and release from machine.

TO JOIN RIGHT SHOULDER
Push 46 Ns to WP. With K side of right back shoulder facing, replace sts on to Ns. Unravel WY. With P side of right front shoulder facing, replace sts on to same Ns. Unravel WY. Using MT and MC, K 1 row. Cast off (bind off).

111

NECKBAND
Machines with ribber
With ribber in position and carriage at right, set machine for 1×1 rib. Using MC, cast on 140 sts in 1×1 nb. K 3 tubular rows. Carriage is at right. Set carriage for 1×1 rib knitting. Set RC at 000. Using MT-6/MT-6, K 24 rows. Transfer sts for st st. With P side facing, pick up sts around neck edge and place on to Ns. Using MT, K 1 row. Cast off (bind off).
Machines without ribber
Push 140 Ns to WP. With K side facing, pick up 140 sts around neck edge and place on to Ns. Set RC at 000. Using MT and MC, K 1 row. Transfer every 3rd st on to adjacent N and push empty Ns to NWP. Using MT-1, K 4 rows. Using MT-2, K 11 rows. Using MT-1, K 3 rows. Push Ns from NWP to WP and place loops from row below adjacent st on to empty Ns. Using MT, K 2 rows. Using WY, K a few rows and release from machine.

TO JOIN LEFT SHOULDER
Work as for right shoulder, reading left for right.

TO JOIN SLEEVES TO ARMHOLES
Push 172 Ns to WP. With K side facing, replace 172 sts from top of sleeve on to Ns. Unravel WY. With P side facing, pick up 172 sts along side edge of armhole and place on to same Ns. Using MT and MC, K 1 row. Cast off (bind off).

PRESSING
With wrong side facing, pin out to measurements given. Press carefully following instructions on cone band.

MAKING UP
Sew rows above markers on sleeves to cast off (bound off) sts on back and front. Join side, sleeve and neckband seams.
Machines with ribber
Fold neckband in half to inside and stipstitch down.
Machines without ribber
Fold neckband in half to outside and pin in position. Unravelling WY as required, backstitch through open loops of last row worked in MC.

Oak Leaf

This Oak Leaf sleeveless cardigan has a plain
back with fine ribs, two small pockets and an optional half belt.

PATTERN RATING
● ● ● For fairly experienced knitters.

MACHINES
This pattern is suitable for standard gauge
punchcard/electronic machines.

MATERIALS
Rowan Fine Fleck Tweed.
150 [175, 200] g (5½ [6½, 7] oz) in shade 62
(MC).
75 [100, 125] g (3 [4, 5] oz) in shade 82 (C).
5 buttons.
Buckle, if required.
2 buttons for belt, if required.
*Rowan Fine Fleck Tweed is 75% Pure New
Wool base, 15% Cotton Nepp, 10% Nylon.*

YARN THICKNESS
Medium yarn.

MEASUREMENTS
To fit chest 76-82 [87-92, 97-102] cm, 30-32
[34-36, 38-40] in.
Actual measurement 91 [101, 111] cm, 35¾
[39¾, 43¾] in.
Length to shoulder 47.5 [49.5, 51.5] cm, 18¾
[19½, 20¼] in.
*Instructions are written for the smallest size,
larger sizes follow in square brackets. If only
one figure is given, it applies to all sizes.*

TENSION
28.5 stitches and 38.5 rows to 10 cm, 4 in

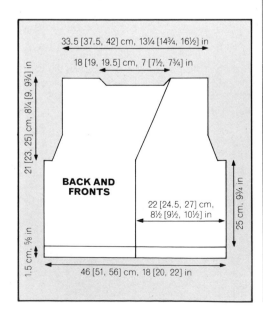

measured over stocking stitch and Fair Isle
patt (tension dial setting approximately 7).
*For perfect results, your tension must be
matched exactly before starting the
garment.*

ABBREVIATIONS
See page 9.

NOTES
Knit side of knitting is right side of finished
garment.
Electronic machines
Fill in pattern card shown on page 114 before
starting to knit. Centre pattern over centre 0.
Punchcard machines
The following card should be punched, if
required, before starting to knit.

BACK
Machines with ribber
With ribber in position and carriage at right,
set machine for 1×1 rib. Using MC, cast on
132 [146, 160] sts in 1×1 rib. K 3 tubular
rows. Carriage is at right. Set carriage for
1×1 rib knitting. Set RC at 000. Using
MT-6/MT-6, K 10 rows. Transfer sts for st st.
Machines without ribber
Push 131 [146, 158] Ns to WP. Push every 3rd
N back to NWP. Using MT and WY, cast on
and K a few rows ending with carriage at
left. Set RC at 000. Using MT-2 and MC, K
15 rows. Push Ns from NWP to WP and
make a hem by placing loops of first row
worked in MC evenly along the row. Unravel
WY when work is completed. Inc 1 [0, 2] sts.
132 [146, 160] sts.
All machines
Set RC at 000. Using MT, K 96 rows. Work
measures 26.5 cm, 10½ in.
Shape armholes Cast off (bind off) 10 sts at
beg of next 2 rows. Dec 1 st at each end of
next and every foll alt row until 96 [108, 120]
sts rem. K 59 [65, 71] rows.
Shape neck Using a length of MC, cast off
(bind off) centre 48 [50, 52] sts. Push 24 [29,
34] Ns at left to HP and cont on rem sts for
first side.
K 1 row. Dec 1 st at beg of next and foll alt
row. 22 [27, 32] sts.
K 2 rows. Using WY, K a few rows and
release from machine.
With carriage at left, push Ns from HP to
UWP and finish to correspond with first side
reversing shapings.

RIGHT FRONT
Machines with ribber
With ribber in position and carriage at right,
set machine for 1×1 rib. Push 32 [35, 39] Ns
at left and right of centre 0 to WP. 64 [70, 78]
Ns. Push corresponding Ns on ribber to WP.
Arrange Ns for 1×1 rib. Using MC, cast on
and K 3 tubular rows. Carriage is at right.
Insert card and lock on first row. Set
carriage for 1×1 rib knitting. Set RC at 000.
Using MT-6/MT-6, K 10 rows. Transfer sts for
st st.
Machines without ribber
Push 31 [34, 39] Ns at left and 31 [34, 38] Ns
at right of centre 0 to WP. 62 [68, 77] Ns.
Push every 3rd N back to NWP. Using MT
and WY, cast on and K a few rows ending
with carriage at left. Insert card and lock on
first row. Set RC at 000. Using MT-2 and
MC, K 15 rows. Push Ns from NWP to WP and
make a hem by placing loops of first
row worked in MC evenly along the row.
Unravel WY when work is completed.
1st and 2nd sizes Inc 1 st at each end.
3rd size Inc 1 st at right edge.
All sizes 64 [70, 78] sts.
All machines
Set RC at 000. Using MT and C, K 1 row.
Release card and cont in Fair Isle patt with C
in feeder 1(A) and MC in feeder 2(B), K 95
rows. RC shows 96 and work measures 26.5
cm, 10½ in. K 1 row extra for left front.
Shape armhole Cast off (bind off) 10 sts at
beg of next row, K 1 row. Dec 1 st at beg of
next and every foll alt row until 46 [51, 58] sts
rem. K 15 [13, 11] rows.
Shape front edge Dec 1 st at front edge of
next and every foll alt row until 22 [27, 32] sts
rem. K 1 [9, 13] rows. Cont in st st and C, K
2 rows. Using WY, K a few rows and release
from machine.

LEFT FRONT
Work as for right front reversing shapings by
noting alteration in number of rows worked.

POCKETS
Push 16 Ns at left and right of centre 0 to
WP. 32 Ns. Insert card and lock on first row.
Using MT and WY, cast on and K a few rows
ending with carriage at right. Set RC at 000.

*The Squares man's sweater and Oak Leaf
woman's sleeveless cardigan are ideal for
extra warmth on a cold winter's day.*

Using C, K 1 row. Release card and cont in Fair Isle patt with C in feeder 1(A) and MC in feeder 2(B), K 32 rows. Using WY, K a few rows in st st and release from machine.

POCKET TOPS
Machines with ribber
With ribber in position and carriage at right, set machine for 1×1 rib. Using MC, cast on 32 sts in 1×1 rib. K 3 tubular rows. Carriage is at right. Set carriage for 1×1 rib knitting. Set RC at 000. Using MT-6/MT-6, K 5 rows. Transfer sts for st st.

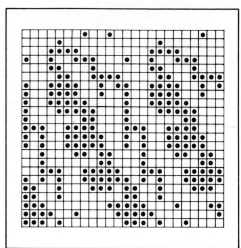

114

Machines without ribber
Push 32 Ns to WP. Push every 3rd N back to NWP. Using MT and WY, cast on and K a few rows ending with carriage at left. Set RC at 000. Using MT-2 and MC, K 9 rows. Push Ns from NWP to WP and make a hem by placing loops of first row worked in MC evenly along the row. Unravel WY when work is completed.
All machines
With P side of pocket facing, replace sts from last row below WY on to Ns. Using MT, K 1 row. Cast off (bind off).

TO JOIN RIGHT SHOULDER
Push 22 [27, 32] Ns to WP. With K side of right back shoulder facing, replace sts on to Ns. Unravel WY. With P side of right front shoulder facing, replace sts on to same Ns. Unravel WY. Using MT and MC, K 1 row. Cast off (bind off).

TO JOIN LEFT SHOULDER
Work as for right shoulder, reading left for right.

ARMHOLE BANDS
Machines with ribber
With ribber in position and carriage at right, set machine for 1×1 rib. Using MC, cast on 136 [150, 164] sts in 1×1 rib. K 3 tubular rows. Carriage is at right. Set carriage for 1×1 rib knitting. Set RC at 000. Using MT-6/MT-6, K 22 rows. Transfer sts for st st. With P side facing, pick up 136 [150, 164] sts around armhole edge and place on to Ns. Using MT, K 1 row. Cast off (bind off).

Machines without ribber
Push 137 [152, 167] Ns to WP. With K side facing, pick up 137 [152, 167] sts around armhole edge and place on to Ns. Set RC at 000. Using MT and MC, K 1 row. Transfer every 3rd st on to adjacent N and push empty Ns to NWP. Using MT-1, K 3 rows. Using MT-2, K 9 rows. Using MT-1, K 2 rows. Push Ns from NWP to WP and place loop from row below adjacent st on to empty Ns. Using MT, K 2 rows. Using WY, K a few rows and release from machine.

BUTTONHOLE BAND
Machines with ribber
With ribber in position and carriage at right, set machine for 1×1 rib. Using MC, cast on 162 [170, 178] sts in 1×1 rib. K 3 tubular rows. Carriage is at right. Set carriage for 1×1 rib knitting. Set RC at 000. Using MT-6/MT-6, K 5 rows. Counting from left edge make buttonholes over 4th, 26th, 48th, 70th and 92nd sts. K 12 rows. Make buttonholes over same sts as before. K 5 rows. Transfer sts for st st. With P side facing, pick up sts along right or left front edge to centre back neck and place on to Ns. Using MT, K 1 row. Cast off (bind off).
Machines without ribber
Push 162 [170, 178] Ns to WP. With K side facing, pick up 162 [170, 178] sts along right or left front edge to centre back neck and place on to Ns. Set RC at 000. Using MT and MC, K 4 rows. Counting from right edge make buttonholes over 4th, 5th; 26th, 27th; 48th, 49th; 70th, 71st; 92nd and 93rd sts. K 9 rows. Make buttonholes over same sts as before. K 4 rows. Using WY, K a few rows and release from machine.

BUTTON BAND
Work as for buttonhole band omitting buttonholes and reading left front for right front or right front for left front.

HALF BELT (Optional)
Machines with ribber
First piece With ribber in position and carriage at right, set machine for 1×1 rib.

Using MC, cast on 15 sts in 1×1 rib. K 3 tubular rows. Carriage is at right. Set carriage for 1×1 rib knitting. Set RC at 000 *. Using MT-6/MT-6, K 120 [130, 140] rows. Transfer sts to back bed. Cast off (bind off).
Second piece Work as for first piece to *. Using MT-6/MT-6, K 100 [110, 120] rows. Transfer sts to back bed. Cast off (bind off).
Machines without ribber
First piece Using MC, cast on 15 sts by hand. Set RC at 000 *.
Using MT, K 114 [124, 134] rows. Cast off (bind off).
Second Piece Work as for first piece to *. Using MT, K 90 [100, 110] rows. Cast off (bind off).

PRESSING
With the wrong side facing, pin out to the measurements given. Press carefully following instructions on cone band.

MAKING UP
WAISTCOAT WITH BELT
Machines without ribber
Fold belt pieces in half lengthways and join seam, neaten ends.
All machines
Join side seams, inserting belt approximately 8 cm, 3¼ in above welt. Sew buckle to shorter belt piece. Attach buttons to hold belt in place.
WAISTCOAT WITHOUT BELT
Join side seams.
BOTH VERSIONS
Sew pockets into position matching pattern and grafting lower edge. Join centre back seam in front bands.
Machines with ribber
Fold armhole bands and front bands in half to inside and slipstitch down.
Machines without ribber
Fold armhole bands and front bands in half to right side and pin in position. Unravelling WY as required, backstitch through open loops of last row worked in MC.
All machines
Finish buttonholes and sew on buttons.

Woman's Work

Women are 50 per cent of the world's population, do two-thirds of the world's work, receive 10 per cent of the world's income, and own less than 1 per cent of the world's property. Most of the work done by women is invisible, often going undervalued, unrecognized and unpaid – domestic work, alongside often additional work outside the home. The four titles in this section – Washing Up, Cleaning Up, Ironing Out and Maternity Leave – take a humorous look at aspects of this work, adding to the literal interpretation of sweaters patterned with teacups, vacuum cleaners, irons and spirals.

Vacuum cleaners and irons designed in the Forties and Fifties have a nostalgic fascination for me, and this was my starting point. Cleaning Up is a direct play on one aspect of the reality of woman's work. The cartoon simplicity of the archetypal domestic vacuum cleaner makes an amusing sweater, especially when worn by a man. The random dots between the vacuum cleaners solve the back-float problem, and also associate it with the Fifties stylistic period.

Ironing Out is a graphic treatment of the chrome-and-black streamlined classic iron; it produces an animated effect with the lines between the motifs suggesting movement or, more literally, cloth.

Maternity Leave is another aspect of woman's work – child-rearing – in a more subtle way. A simple embryonic spiral creates a paisley effect which keeps the connotations of the title Maternity Leave suitably ambiguous. This sweater is knitted in off-white and black, but a more restrained effect could be achieved using beige and black.

The association between polka-dot china teacups and washing up is a nostalgic return to my own childhood, and the polka dots create a cohesive rhythm among the flying crockery. The collar produces an alternative neck detail; it could be adapted for other sweaters in this section.

All the sweaters in Woman's Work could be made in cotton for spring, but they are more successful if the patterning remains black or a very dark colour. Despite the use of dots and lines between the motifs, the back-floats may cause concern. You could loosely stitch up the back of the sleeve floats, but on the body pieces it's probably not necessary.

We chose to photograph Woman's Work against the beautiful industrial façade of Wallis Gilbert's Hoover Building, situated in the suburbs of West London on the road to Oxford. This Art Deco building is an inspiration in itself and, in the context of this section, represents the dual nature of woman's work – both in domestic and work settings.

Washing Up

This expressive polka dot cup design creates the impression of flying crockery. The collar gives an alternative neck detail.

116 PATTERN RATING
● ● Fairly easy; for knitters with some experience.

MACHINES
This pattern is suitable for electronic machines.

MATERIALS
Rowan Botany Wool.
325 g (12 oz) in shade 633 (MC).
212 g (8 oz) in shade 62 (C).
Rowan Botany Wool is 100% Pure New Wool.

YARN THICKNESS
Medium yarn.

MEASUREMENTS
To fit chest 92cm, 36in.
Actual measurement 119 cm, 46¾ in.
Length to shoulder 54 cm, 21¼ in.
Sleeve seam 46 cm, 18¼ in.

TENSION
31 sts and 39 rows to 10 cm, 4 in measured over Fair Isle pattern (tension dial setting approximately 7).
For perfect results, your tension must be matched exactly before starting the garment.

ABBREVIATIONS
See page 9.

NOTES
Knit side of knitting is right side of finished garment. Fill in pattern card, shown on page 118, before starting to knit.

BACK
Machines with ribber
With ribber in position and carriage at right, set machine for 1×1 rib. Push 87 Ns at left and right of centre 0 to WP. 174 Ns.
* Push corresponding Ns on ribber to WP. Arrange Ns for 1×1 rib. Using MC, cast on and K 3 tubular rows. Carriage is at right. Insert card and lock on first row. Set carriage for 1×1 rib knitting. Set RC at 000. Using MT-6/MT-6, K 14 rows. Transfer sts for st st *.

Machines without ribber
Push 87 Ns at left and 86 Ns at right of centre 0 to WP. 173 Ns.
* Push every 3rd N back to NWP. Using MT and WY, cast on and K a few rows ending with carriage at left. Insert card and lock on first row. Set RC at 000. Using MT-2 and MC, K 19 rows. Push Ns from NWP to WP and make a hem by placing loops of first row worked in MC evenly along the row. Unravel WY when work is completed *.
Inc 1 st at right edge. 174 sts.

All machines
Set RC at 000. Using MT, K 1 row. Release card and cont in Fair Isle patt with MC in feeder 1(A) and C in feeder 2(B). K 8 rows. Shape sides by inc 1 st at each end of next and every foll 10th row until there are 186 sts. K 26 rows. RC shows 86 and work measures 24 cm, 9½ in.
Shape armholes Cast off (bind off) 15 sts at beg of next 2 rows. 156 sts **.
K 110 rows.
Shape neck Note patt row on card. Using a length of MC, cast off (bind off) centre 56 sts. Using nylon cord, K 50 sts at left by hand taking Ns down to NWP. Cont on rem sts for first side. K 1 row. Dec 1 st at beg of next and foll alt row. 48 sts. Cont in st st and MC. K 2 rows. Using WY, K a few rows and release from machine.
With carriage at right, unravel nylon cord over rem Ns bringing Ns back to WP. Lock card on number previously noted. Take carriage to left without knitting. Release card and cont in Fair Isle patt. Finish to correspond with first side reversing shapings.

FRONT
Work as for Back to **.
K 86 rows.
Shape neck Note patt row on card. Place a marker at centre 0. Using a length of MC, cast off (bind off) centre 34 sts. Using nylon cord, K 61 sts at left by hand taking Ns down to NWP.
Cont on rem sts for first side.
K 1 row. Dec 1 st at beg of next and every foll alt row until 48 sts rem. K 2 rows. Cont in st st and MC. K 2 rows. Using WY, K a few rows and release from machine.
With carriage at right, unravel nylon cord over rem Ns bringing Ns back to WP. Lock card on number previously noted. Take carriage to left without knitting. Release card and cont in Fair Isle patt. Finish to correspond with first side reversing shapings.

SLEEVES
Machines with ribber
With ribber in position and carriage at right, set machine for 1×1 rib. Push 37 Ns at left and right of centre 0 to WP. 74 Ns. Work as for Back from * to *.
Machines without ribber
Push 37 Ns at left and right of centre 0 to WP. 74 Ns. Work as for Back from * to *.
All machines
Set RC at 000. Using MT. K 1 row. Release

They say that a woman's work is never done but the teacups on this sweater will never need Washing Up. If preferred knit a ribbed neckband instead of the collar.

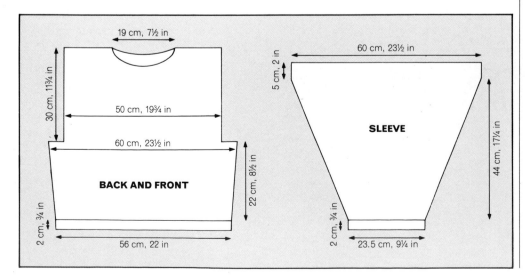

19 cm, 7½ in
30 cm, 11¾ in
50 cm, 19¾ in
60 cm, 23½ in
BACK AND FRONT
2 cm, ¾ in
22 cm, 8½ in
56 cm, 22 in

60 cm, 23½ in
5 cm, 2 in
SLEEVE
44 cm, 17¼ in
2 cm, ¾ in
23.5 cm, 9¼ in

card and cont in Fair Isle patt with MC in feeder 1(A) and C in feeder 2(B). K 1 row. Shape sides by inc 1 st at each end of next and every foll 3rd row until there are 186 sts. K 4 rows. RC shows 172 and work measures 46 cm, 18¼ in. Place marker at each end. K 18 rows. Cont in st st and MC. K 2 rows. Using WY, K a few rows and release from machine.

COLLAR
Machines with ribber
With ribber in position and carriage at right, set machine for 1×1 rib. Using MC, cast on 160 sts in 1×1 rib. K 3 tubular rows. Carriage is at right. Set carriage for 1×1 rib knitting. Set RC at 000. Using MT-6/MT-6, K 58 rows. Transfer sts for st st. Using WY, K a few rows and release from machine.

Machines without ribber
Push 161 Ns to WP. Push every 3rd N back to NWP. Using MT and WY, cast on and K a few rows ending with carriage at right. Set RC at 000. Using MT-2 and MC, K 81 rows. Push Ns from NWP to WP and make a hem by placing loops of first row worked in MC evenly along the row. Unravel WY when work is completed. Using MT, K 2 rows. Using WY, K a few rows and release from machine.

TO JOIN RIGHT SHOULDER
Push 48 Ns to WP. With K side of right back shoulder facing, replace sts on to Ns. Unravel WY. With P side of right shoulder facing, replace sts on to same Ns. Unravel WY. Using MT and MC, K 1 row. Cast off (bind off).

TO JOIN LEFT SHOULDER
Work as for right shoulder, reading left for right.

TO JOIN SLEEVES TO ARMHOLES
Push 186 Ns to WP. With K side facing, replace 186 sts from top of sleeve on to Ns. Unravel WY. With P side facing, pick up 186 sts along side edge of armhole and place on to same Ns. Using MT and MC, K 1 row. Cast off (bind off).

PRESSING
With wrong side facing, pin out to measurements given. Press carefully following instructions on cone or ball band.

MAKING UP
Sew rows above markers on sleeves to cast off (bound off) sts on back and front. Join side and sleeve seams.
Pin the collar into position with the ends at marker. Unravelling WY as required, backstitch through open loops of last row worked in MC.
Machines without ribber
Neaten ends of collar.
All machines
Join the row ends of the collar at centre front neck for 2.5 cm, 1 in.

Cleaning Up

The archetypal domestic vacuum cleaner
of the '50s was the inspiration for this pattern.

PATTERN RATING
●● Fairly easy; for knitters with some experience.

MACHINES
This pattern is suitable for electronic machines.

MATERIALS
Rowan Botany Wool.
390 g (14 oz) in shade 420 (MC).
250 g (9 oz) in shade 62 (C).
Rowan Botany Wool is 100% Pure New Wool.

YARN THICKNESS
Medium yarn.

MEASUREMENTS
To fit chest 102 cm, 40 in.

Actual measurement 117 cm, 46 in.
Length to shoulder 65 cm, 25½ in.
Sleeve seam 54 cm, 21¼ in.

TENSION
31 stitches and 39 rows to 10 cm, 4 in measured over Fair Isle pattern (tension dial setting approximately 7).
For perfect results, your tension must be matched exactly before starting the garment.

ABBREVIATIONS
See page 9.

NOTES
Knit side of knitting is right side of finished garment. Fill in pattern card, shown on page 121, before starting to knit.

BACK
Machines with ribber
With ribber in position and carriage at right, set machine for 1×1 rib. Push 87 Ns at left and right of centre 0 to WP. 174 Ns. * Push corresponding Ns on ribber to WP. Arrange Ns for 1×1 rib. Using MC, cast on and K 3 tubular rows. Carriage is at right. Insert card and lock on first row. Set carriage for 1×1 rib knitting. Set RC at 000. Using MT-6/MT-6, K 26 rows. Transfer sts for st st *.
Machines without ribber
Push 87 Ns at left and 86 Ns at right of centre 0 to WP. 173 Ns.

After Washing Up comes Cleaning Up. This man's sweater is covered with motifs of the classic vacuum cleaner.

* Push every 3rd N back to NWP. Using MT and WY, cast on and K a few rows ending with carriage at left. Insert card and lock on first row. Set RC at 000. Using MT-2 and MC, K 37 rows. Push Ns from NWP to WP and make a hem by placing loops of first row worked in MC evenly along the row. Unravel WY when work is completed *. Inc 1 st at right edge. 174 sts.

All machines
Set RC at 000. Using MT, K 1 row. Release card and cont in Fair Isle patt with MC in feeder 1(A) and C in feeder 2(B). K 18 rows. Shape sides by inc 1 st at each end of next and every foll 20th row until there are 184 sts. K 30 rows. RC shows 130 and work measures 37 cm, 14½ in.

Shape armholes Cast off (bind off) 15 sts at beg of next 2 rows. 154 sts **.
K 102 rows.

Shape neck Note patt row on card. Using a length of MC, cast off (bind off) centre 58 sts. Using nylon cord, K 48 sts at left by hand taking Ns down to NWP. Cont on rem sts for first side. K 1 row. Dec 1 st at beg of next and foll alt row. 46 sts. Cont in st st and MC. K 2 rows. Using WY, K a few rows and release from machine.
With carriage at right, unravel nylon cord over rem Ns bringing Ns back to WP. Lock card on number previously noted. Take carriage to left without knitting. Release card and cont in Fair Isle patt. Finish to correspond with first side reversing shapings.

FRONT
Work as for Back to **. K 80 rows.
Shape neck Note patt row on card. Using a length of MC, cast off (bind off) centre 36 sts. Using nylon cord K 59 sts at left by hand taking Ns down to NWP. Cont on rem sts for first side. K 1 row. Dec 1 st at beg of next and every foll alt row until 46 sts rem. Cont in st st and MC. K 2 rows. Using WY, K a few rows and release from machine.
With carriage at right, unravel nylon cord over rem Ns bringing Ns back to WP. Lock card on number previously noted. Take carriage to left without knitting. Release card and cont in Fair Isle patt. Finish to correspond with first side reversing shapings.

SLEEVES
Machines with ribber
With ribber in position and carriage at right, set machine for 1×1 rib. Push 38 Ns at left and right of centre 0 to WP. 76 Ns. Work as for Back from * to *.
Machines without ribber
Push 37 Ns at left and right of centre 0 to WP. 74 Ns. Work as for Back from * to *. Inc. 1 st at each end. 76 sts.
All machines
Set RC at 000. Using MT, K 1 row. Release card and cont in Fair Isle patt with MC in feeder 1(A) and C in feeder 2(B). Shape sides by inc 1 st at each end of next and every foll 4th row until there are 174 sts. K 1 row. RC shows 195 and work measures 54 cm, 21¼

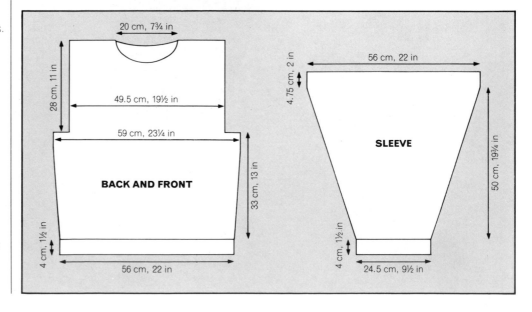

BACK AND FRONT

20 cm, 7¾ in
28 cm, 11 in
49.5 cm, 19½ in
59 cm, 23¼ in
33 cm, 13 in
4 cm, 1½ in
56 cm, 22 in

SLEEVE

4.75 cm, 2 in
56 cm, 22 in
50 cm, 19¾ in
4 cm, 1½ in
24.5 cm, 9½ in

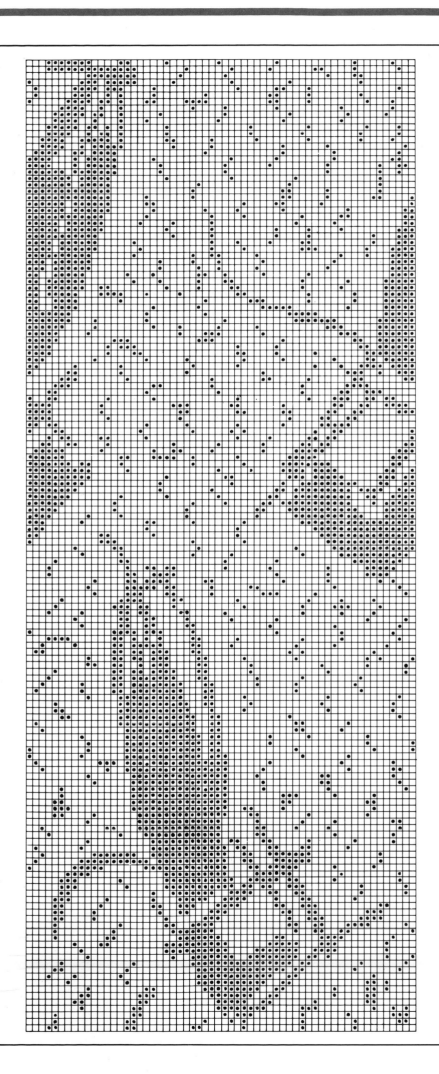

in. Place marker at each end. K 17 rows. Cont in st st and MC. K 2 rows. Using WY, K a few rows and release from machine.

TO JOIN RIGHT SHOULDER

Push 46 Ns to WP. With K side of right back shoulder facing, replace sts on to Ns. Unravel WY. With P side of right front shoulder facing, replace sts on to same Ns. Unravel WY. Using MT and MC, K 1 row. Cast off (bind off).

NECKBAND

Machines with ribber

With ribber in position and carriage at right, set machine for 1×1 rib. Using MC, cast on 150 sts in 1×1 rib. K 3 tubular rows. Carriage is at right. Set carriage for 1×1 rib knitting. Set RC at 000.
Using MT-6/MT-6, K 30 rows. Transfer sts for st st. Using WY, K a few rows and release from machine.

Machines without ribber

Push 152 Ns to WP. With K side facing, pick up 152 sts around neck edge and place on to Ns. Set RC at 000.
Using MT and MC, K 1 row. Transfer every 3rd st on to adjacent N and push empty Ns to NWP.
Using MT-1, K 5 rows. Using MT-2, K 11 rows. Using MT-1, K 4 rows. Push Ns from NWP to WP and place loop from row below adjacent st on to empty N. Using MT, K 2 rows. Using WY, K a few rows and release from machine.

TO JOIN LEFT SHOULDER

Work as for right shoulder, reading left for right.

TO JOIN SLEEVES TO ARMHOLES

Push 174 Ns to WP. With K side facing, replace 174 sts from top of sleeve on to Ns. Unravel WY.
With the P side facing, pick up 174 sts along side edge of armhole and place on to the same Ns. Using MT and MC, K 1 row. Cast off (bind off).

PRESSING

With wrong side facing, pin out to measurements given. Press carefully following instructions on cone or ball band.

MAKING UP

Sew rows above markers on sleeves to cast off (bound off) sts on back and front. Join side and sleeve seams. Join neckband seam.

Machines with ribber

Pin neckband in position. Unravelling WY as required, backstitch through open loops of last row worked in MC. Fold in half and slipstitch down on inside.

Machines without ribber

Fold neckband in half to outside and pin in position. Unravelling WY as required, backstitch through open loops of last row worked in MC.

Maternity Leave

A simple embryonic spiral creates a Paisley effect, keeping
its light-hearted title ambiguous.

PATTERN RATING
● ● *Fairly easy; for knitters with some experience.*

MACHINES
This pattern is suitable for standard gauge punchcard/electronic machines.

MATERIALS
Rowan Botany Wool.
425 g (15 oz) in shade 1 (MC).
265 g (10 oz) in shade 62 (C).
Rowan Botany Wool is 100% Pure New Wool.

YARN THICKNESS
Medium yarn.

MEASUREMENTS
To fit chest 87-97 cm, 34-38 in.
Actual measurement 125 cm, 49¼ in.
Length to shoulder 79 cm, 31 in.
Sleeve seam 45.75 cm, 18 in.

TENSION
31 sts and 39 rows to 10 cm, 4 in measured over Fair Isle pattern (tension dial setting approximately 7).
For perfect results, tension must be matched exactly before starting the garment.

ABBREVIATIONS
See page 9.

NOTES
Knit side of knitting is right side of finished garment.
Punchcard machines
Punch the card, shown on page 124, before starting to knit.
Electronic machines
Fill in pattern card before starting to knit.

BACK
Machines with ribber
With ribber in position and carriage at right, set machine for 1×1 rib. Push 90 Ns at left and right of centre 0 to WP. 180 Ns.
* Push corresponding Ns on ribber to WP. Arrange Ns for 1×1 rib. Using MC, cast on and K 3 tubular rows. Carriage is at right. Insert card and lock on first row. Set carriage for 1×1 rib knitting. Set RC at 000. Using MT-6/MT-6, K 14 rows. Transfer sts for st st *.
Machines without ribber
Push 90 Ns at left and 89 Ns at right of centre 0 to WP. 179 Ns.
* Push every 3rd N back to NWP. Using MT and WY, cast on and K a few rows ending with carriage at left. Insert card and lock on first row.
Set RC at 000. Using MT-2 and MC, K 27 rows. Push Ns from NWP to WP and make a hem by placing loops of first row worked in MC evenly along the row. Unravel WY when work is completed *.
Inc 1 st at right edge. 180 sts.
All machines
Set RC at 000. Using MT, K 1 row. Release card and cont in Fair Isle patt with MC in feeder 1(A) and C in feeder 2(B). K 18 rows. Shape sides by inc 1 st at each end of next and every foll 20th row until there are 196 sts. K 20 rows. RC shows 180 and work measures 49 cm, 19¼ in.
Shape armholes Cast off (bind off) 15 sts at

Maternity Leave, a loose fitting sweater covered with small embryonic motifs, is seen here with Ironing Out and Cleaning Up sweaters. Knit them with any colour background and black outlined motifs.

beg of next 2 rows. 166 sts **. K 110 rows.
Shape neck Note patt row on card. Using a length of MC, cast off (bind off) centre 58 sts. Using nylon cord, K 54 sts at left by hand taking Ns down to NWP. Cont on rem sts for first side. K 1 row. Dec 1 st at beg of next and foll alt row. 52 sts. Cont in st st and MC. K 2 rows. Using WY, K a few rows and release from machine.
With carriage at right, unravel nylon cord over rem Ns bringing Ns back to WP. Lock card on number previously noted. Take carriage to left without knitting. Release card and cont in Fair Isle patt. Finish to correspond with first side reversing shapings. **123**

FRONT
Work as for Back to **.
K 48 rows.
Shape neck Note patt row on card. Using nylon cord, K 83 sts at left by hand taking Ns down to NWP. Cont on rem sts for first side. K 1 row. Dec 1 st at beg of next and every foll alt row until 52 sts rem. K 4 rows. Cont in st st and MC. K 2 rows. Using WY, K a few rows and release from machine.
With carriage at right, unravel nylon cord over rem Ns bringing Ns back to WP. Lock card on number previously noted. Take carriage to left without knitting. Release card and cont in Fair Isle patt. Finish to correspond with first side reversing shapings.

SLEEVES
Machines with ribber
With ribber in position and carriage at right, set machine for 1×1 rib. Push 37 Ns at left and right of centre 0 to WP. 74 Ns. Work as for Back from * to *.
Machines without ribber
Push 37 Ns at left and right of centre 0 to WP. 74 Ns. Work as for Back from * to *.
All machines
Set RC at 000. Using MT, K 1 row. Release card and cont in Fair Isle patt with MC in feeder 1(A) and C in feeder 2(B). Shape sides by inc 1 st at each end of next and every foll 3rd row until there are 186 sts. RC shows 167 and work measures 45.75 cm, 18 in. Place marker at each end. K 17 rows. Cont in st st and MC. K 2 rows. Using WY, K a few rows and release from machine.

NECKBAND
Machines with ribber
With ribber in position and carriage at right, set machine for 1×1 rib. Using MC, cast on 180 sts in 1×1 rib. K 3 tubular rows. Carriage is at right. Set carriage for 1×1 rib knitting. Set RC at 000. Using MT-6/MT-6, K 25 rows. Transfer sts for st st. Using WY, K a few rows and release from machine.
Machines without ribber
Push 179 Ns to WP. Push every 3rd N back to NWP. Using MT and WY, cast on and K a few rows ending with carriage at right. Set RC at 000. Using MT-2 and MC, K 23 rows. Push Ns from NWP to WP and make a hem by placing loops of first row worked in MC

BACK AND FRONT

20 cm, 7¾ in

30 cm, 11¾ in

53.5 cm, 21 in

63 cm, 24¾ in

46 cm, 18 in

3 cm, 1¼ in

58 cm, 22¾ in

SLEEVE

60 cm, 23½ in

4.75 cm, 2 in

42.75 cm, 17 in

3 cm, 1¼ in

23. 5 cm, 9¼ in

evenly along the row. Unravel WY when work is completed. Using MT, K 2 rows. Using WY, K a few rows and release from machine.

TO JOIN RIGHT SHOULDER

Push 52 Ns to WP. With K side of right back shoulder facing, replace sts on to Ns. Unravel WY. With P side of right front shoulder facing, replace sts on to same Ns. Unravel WY. Using MT and MC, K 1 row. Cast off (bind off).

TO JOIN LEFT SHOULDER

Work as for right shoulder, reading left for right.

TO JOIN SLEEVES TO ARMHOLES

Push 186 Ns to WP. With K side facing, replace 186 sts from top of sleeve on to Ns. Unravel WY. With P side facing, pick up 186 sts along side edge of armhole and place on to same Ns. Using MT and MC, K 1 row. Cast off (bind off).

PRESSING

With wrong side facing, pin out to the measurements given. Press carefully following instructions on cone or ball band.

MAKING UP

Sew rows above markers on sleeves to cast off (bound off) sts on back and front. Join side and sleeve seams. Pin neckband in position. Unravelling WY as required, backstitch through open loops of last row worked in MC.

Machines with ribber

Fold the neckband in half to inside and slipstitch down.

All machines

Cross over the ends at centre front and slipstitch down.

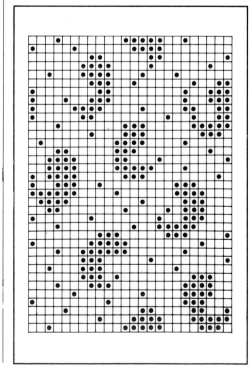

Ironing Out

This graphic treatment of the classic iron gives the sweater its title.

For a more restrained feel, knit this motif sweater with a neutral background colour.

PATTERN RATING
●● Fairly easy; for knitters with some experience.

MACHINES
This pattern is suitable for electronic machines.

MATERIALS
Rowan Botany Wool.
360 g (13 oz) in shade 44 (MC).
195 g (7 oz) in shade 62 (C).
Rowan Botany Wool is 100% Pure New Wool.

YARN THICKNESS
Medium yarn.

MEASUREMENTS
To fit chest 92 cm, 36 in.
Actual measurement 113 cm, 44½ in.
Length to shoulder 66 cm, 26 in.
Sleeve seam 46.5 cm, 18¼ in.

TENSION
31 stitches and 39 rows to 10 cm, 4 in measured over Fair Isle pattern (tension dial setting approximately 7).
For perfect results, your tension must be matched exactly before starting the garment.

ABBREVIATIONS
See page 9.

NOTES
Knit side of knitting is right side of finished garment. Fill in pattern card, shown on page 126, before starting to knit.

BACK
Machines with ribber
With ribber in position and carriage at right, set machine for 1×1 rib. Push 83 Ns at left and right of centre 0 to WP. 166 Ns.
* Push corresponding Ns on ribber to WP. Arrange Ns for 1×1 rib. Using MC, cast on and K 3 tubular rows. Carriage is at right. Insert card and lock on first row. Set carriage for 1×1 rib knitting. Set RC at 000. Using MT-6/MT-6, K 14 rows. Transfer sts for st st *.

Machines without ribber
Push 82 Ns at left and right of centre 0 to WP. 164 Ns.
* Push every 3rd N back to NWP. Using MT

If preferred, swap the Ironing Out and Maternity Leave charts to knit alternative necklines to these stylish sweaters.

and WY, cast on and K a few rows ending with carriage at left. Insert card and lock on first row. Set RC at 000. Using MT-2 and MC, K 19 rows. Push Ns from NWP to WP and make a hem by placing loops of first row worked in MC evenly along the row. Unravel WY when work is completed *.
Inc 1 st at each end. 166 sts.

All machines
Set RC at 000. Using MT, K 1 row. Release card and cont in Fair Isle patt with MC in feeder 1(A) and C in feeder 2(B). K 18 rows. Shape sides by inc 1 st at each end of next and every foll 20th row until there are 178 sts. K 28 rows. RC shows 148 and work measures 40 cm, 15¾ in.
Shape armholes Cast off (bind off) 12 sts at beg of next 2 rows.
154 sts **. K 94 rows.
Shape neck Note patt row on card. Using a length of MC, cast off (bind off) centre 56

sts. Using nylon cord, K 49 sts at left by hand taking Ns down to NWP. Cont on rem sts for first side.
K 1 row. Dec 1 st at beg of next and foll alt row. 47 sts. Cont in st st and MC.
K 2 rows. Using WY, K a few rows and release from machine.
With carriage at right, unravel nylon cord over rem Ns bringing Ns back to WP. Lock card on number previously noted. Take carriage to left without knitting. Release card and cont in Fair Isle patt. Finish to correspond with first side reversing shapings.

FRONT
Work as for Back to **.
K 72 rows.

Shape neck Note patt row on card. Using a length of MC, cast off (bind off) centre 34 sts. Using nylon cord, K 60 sts at left by hand taking Ns down to NWP. Cont on rem sts for first side.
K 1 row. Dec 1 st at beg of next and every foll alt row until 47 sts rem. Cont in st st and MC. K 2 rows. Using WY, K a few rows and release from machine.
With carriage at right, unravel nylon cord over rem Ns bringing Ns back to WP. Lock card on number previously noted. Take carriage to left without knitting. Release card and cont in Fair Isle patt. Finish to correspond with first side reversing shaping

SLEEVES
Machines with ribber
With ribber in position and carriage at right, set machine for 1×1 rib. Push 30 Ns at left and right of centre 0 to WP. 60 Ns. Work as for Back from * to *.
Machines without ribber.
Push 30 Ns at left and 29 Ns at right of centre 0 to WP. 59 Ns. Work as for Back from * to *.
Inc 1 st at right edge. 60 sts.
All machines
Set RC at 000. Using MT, K 1 row. Release card and cont in Fair Isle patt with MC in feeder 1(A) and C in feeder 2(B). K 1 row. Shape sides by inc 1 st at each end of next and every foll 3rd row until there are 162 sts. K 21 rows. RC shows 174 and work measures 46.5 cm, 18¼ in. Place marker at each end. K 13 rows. Cont in st st and MC. K 2 rows. Using WY, K a few rows and release from machine.

TO JOIN RIGHT SHOULDER

Push 47 Ns to WP. With K side of right back shoulder facing, replace sts on to Ns. Unravel WY. With P side of right front shoulder facing, replace sts on to same Ns. Unravel WY. Using MT and MC, K 1 row. Cast off (bind off).

NECKBAND

Machines with ribber

With ribber in position and carriage at right, set machine for 1×1 rib. Using MC, cast on 140 sts in 1×1 rib. K 3 tubular rows. Carriage is at right. Set carriage for 1×1 rib knitting. Set RC at 000. Using MT-6/MT-6, K 24 rows. Transfer sts for st st. Using WY, K a few rows and release from machine.

Machines without ribber

Push 140 Ns to WP. With K side facing, pick up 140 sts around neck edge and place on to Ns. Set RC at 000. Using MT and MC, K 1 row. Transfer every 3rd st on to adjacent N and push empty Ns to NWP. Using MT-1, K 4 rows. Using MT-2, K 9 rows. Using MT-1, K 3 rows. Push Ns from NWP to WP and place loop from row below adjacent st on to empty N. Using MT, K 2 rows. Using WY, K a few rows and release from machine.

TO JOIN LEFT SHOULDER

Work as given for right shoulder, reading left instead of right.

126

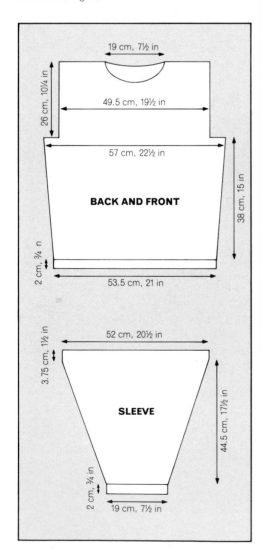

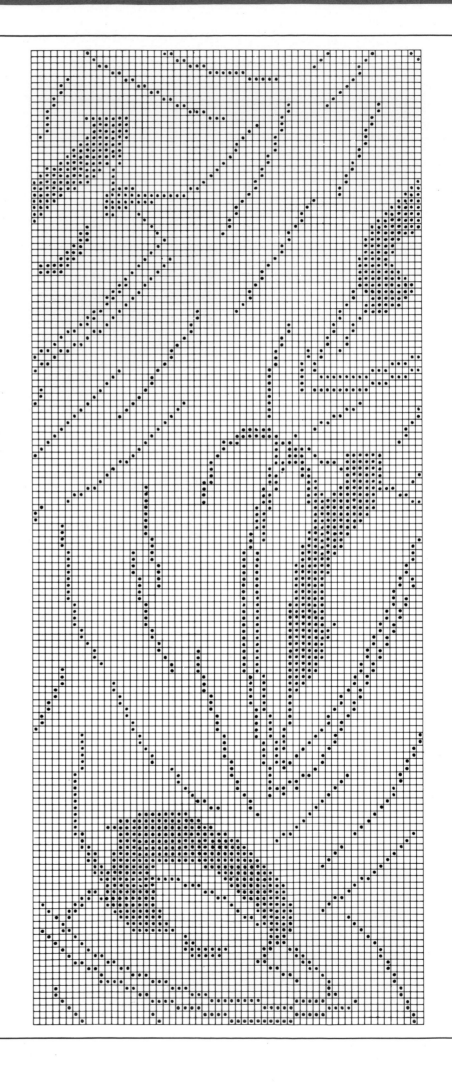

TO JOIN SLEEVES TO ARMHOLES
Push 162 Ns to WP. With K side facing, replace 162 sts from top of sleeve on to Ns. Unravel WY. With P side facing, pick up 162 sts along side edge of armhole and place on to same Ns. Using MT and MC, K 1 row. Cast off (bind off).

PRESSING
With wrong side facing, pin out to the measurements given. Press carefully following instructions on cone or ball band.

MAKING UP
Sew rows above markers on sleeves to cast off sts on back and front. Join side and sleeve seams. Join neckband seam.
Machines with ribber
Pin neckband in position. Unravelling WY as required, backstitch through open loops of last row worked in MC. Fold in half and slipstitch down on inside.
Machines without ribber
Fold neckband in half to right side and pin in position. Unravelling WY as required, backstitch through open loops of last row worked in MC.

Washing Up and Ironing Out humorously symbolize a typical day of a woman's work.

Acknowledgements

128 The author and publisher would like to thank Dick Stringer and Alexandra Karen, as well as the following suppliers for their help with clothes, footwear and accessories:
Ally Capellino, c/o Jean Bennett PR, Macklin Street, London WC2 for shirts and blouses on pages 16, 17, 18, 20, 21, and 29.
Antique Costume & Textile Gallery, Church Street, Marylebone, London NW8 for the floral skirt and sash on pages 95, 97 and 98.
Arkitect, Langley Court, Covent Garden, London WC2 for the man's black wool suit on pages 7, 106 and 108.
Astral Sports, D.H. Evans, Oxford Street, London W1 for the sports equipment on pages 36, 38, 39 and 43.
Chaussures Ravel, c/o Keene PR, Golden Square, London W1 for the shoes on pages 23, 24, 92 and 94.
Detail, Endell Street, Covent Garden, London WC2 for the jewellery on pages 70, 72, 74, 89, 92, 94, 95, 97, 98, 101 and 103.
Georgina Von Etzdorp, Lords, Burlington Arcade, Piccadilly, London W1 for the silk scarves and wraps on pages 106, 109, 110 and 113.
Jigsaw, Long Acre, Covent Garden, London WC2 for the jeans on pages 70, 79 and 89.

Olympus Sport, Oxford Street, London W1 for the sports shoes on pages 33, 35 and 46.
Shelly's Shoes, Oxford Street, London W1 for the footwear on pages 50, 53, 54, 63, 64, 74 and 89.
10/6 Design, Downs Park Road, London E5 for the headwear on pages 68, 70, 72, 74 and 87.
Thomas Kettle, Neal Street, Covent Garden, London WC2 for the watches on pages 16, 17, 18, 20, 21 and 27.
Warehouse, Long Acre, Covent Garden, London WC2 for the accessories on pages 16 and 18; the raffia headwear on pages 79 and 89; and the grey sports vest on pages 36 and 38.

Yarn Suppliers

For details of coned yarn stockists please write to:

UK and Europe
Rowan Yarns, Green Lane Mill, Holmfirth, West Yorkshire HD7 1RW, England
Tel (0484) 686714/687374
S. & J. Andrews Ltd, (trading as Brockwell Wools), Stansfield Mill, Triangle, Halifax, W. Yorkshire HX6 3LZ
Tel (0422) 834 343

USA and Canada
Westminster Trading, 5 Northern Boulevard, Amherst, New Hampshire 03031, USA
Tel (603) 886-5041

New Zealand
Creative Fashion Centre, PO Box 45 083, Epuni Railway, Lower Hutt, New Zealand

Australia
Hutchinson Publishing Group, (Australia) Pty, Ltd, PO Box 496, Hawthorn, Melbourne, Victoria 3122, Australia
Tel (03) 862 3311

South Africa
Jumpers, Admiral's Court, 31 Tyrwhitt Avenue, Rosebank 2196, Johannesburg, South Africa
Tel (011) 788 3798